God,
Just
Tell Me
What to
Do

God, Just Tell Me What to Do

MICHAEL YOUSSEF

HARVEST HOUSE PUBLISHERS
EUGENE, OREGON

Cover design by Left Coast Design, Portland, Oregon

Published in association with the literary agency of Wolgemuth & Associates. Inc.

GOD, JUST TELL ME WHAT TO DO

Copyright © 2014 by Michael Youssef
Published by Harvest House Publishers
Eugene, Oregon 97402
www.harvesthousepublishers.com

Library of Congress Cataloging-in-Publication Data
    Youssef, Michael.
    God, just tell me what to do / Michael Youssef.
      pages cm
    ISBN 978-0-7369-5297-2 (pbk.)
    ISBN 978-0-7369-5298-9 (eBook)
    1. Bible. James—Commentaries. I. Title.
    BS2785.53.Y68 2014
    227'.9107—dc23
                                                            2013045511

*To Roy Anthony Adams
in thanksgiving for thirty years of giving me and my family
faithful and wise counsel and advice.*

Acknowledgments

I am grateful to Jim Denney and Don Gates for using their gifts to help make this book more relevant and practical.

Special thanks to the entire team at Harvest House Publishers—and especially to Bob Hawkins Jr., LaRae Weikert, and Rod Morris, who shared my dream and helped to enlarge the vision of this book.

Finally, thanks to the people of The Church of The Apostles in Atlanta, Georgia, for their constant encouragement and support. They were the first audience for this message, and they helped me to refine the message with their questions and helpful comments.

Contents

A First-Century Letter to Twenty-First-Century Christians

People used to cross the Amargosa Desert in western Nevada on a lonely, seldom-used trail. There was just one spot along the trail where hardy travelers might find drinking water for their journey. At that spot there was an old-fashioned pump with a tin can tied to the handle. Rolled up inside the tin can was a note that read:

> This pump is all right as of June 1932. I put a new sucker washer into it and it ought to last five years. But the washer dries out and the pump has got to be primed. Under the white rock I buried a bottle of water, out of the sun and cork end up. There's enough water in it to prime the pump, but not if you drink some first. Pour about one fourth and let her soak to wet the leather. Then pour in the rest medium-fast and pump like crazy. You'll git water. The well has never run dry. Have faith.

When you git watered up, fill the bottle and put it back
like you found it for the next feller.

(signed) Desert Pete

P.S. Don't go drinking the water first. Prime the pump
with it and you'll git all you can hold.[1]

What do you think Desert Pete means when he says, "Have faith"?

First, Pete is telling the thirsty traveler to believe that there's water
in the well, that the pump will work as promised, and that the well
has never run dry. He's also telling the thirsty traveler to take the risk
of faith, to uncork the bottle of water and to pour every drop into the
pump instead of yielding to the temptation to drink it.

Moreover, Pete is telling the thirsty traveler to take action, to add
work to his faith, to grab the handle and pump it like crazy in order
to bring more water out of the ground. And finally, Pete is telling the
thirsty traveler to refill the bottle, bury it under the white rock, and
leave it as he found it for the next thirsty traveler.

That is what faith means, as it is defined in the book of James.

The book of James is all about having faith, taking risks for that
faith, putting that faith into action, and sharing the refreshment of
authentic faith with others. The book of James is like a well of cool
water in the desert of this harsh, dry life. It's not good enough to
merely believe there's water in the well. We have to prime the pump,
seize the handle, and vigorously put our faith into action.

That's why I've written a book that explores the practical insights
of the book of James. I call this book *God, Just Tell Me What to Do*
because James tells us how to set our beliefs into motion. It tells us,
specifically and concretely, how to transform our *creeds* into *deeds*
day-by-day.

There's nothing theoretical about the book of James. It's filled with
practical advice and insight on how to live for God, whether in the
first century AD or the twenty-first century AD. The book of James
is short enough to read in fifteen or twenty minutes—a perfect length
for today's on-the-go, high-speed-Internet Christians. It's made up of

108 verses into which James has distilled many clear, concise insights for living the life of faith in these difficult times.

These principles will transform our family relationships and friendships, our business relationships and church relationships, and even our interactions on social media. The instructions in the book of James will show us how to live effectively for Christ whether we are rich or poor, successful or struggling, on a spiritual high or in the valley of persecution. If you need comforting, the message of James will sustain you. If you need to be confronted, the message of James will convict you and point you in the right direction. Because James wrote his letter to persecuted first-century believers scattered across the pagan Roman Empire, it still speaks to us today—twenty-first-century believers who are increasingly mocked and hated by the pagan, post-Christian culture that surrounds us. We live in an age of conflict, and James has a message we desperately need to hear.

The book of James challenges the "easy believism" of "churchianity," and urges us to take our faith to a deeper, more dynamic level. Real faith, James says, is demonstrated by action, not mere words. He wants us to know that the only faith that lasts, the only faith that has real meaning, is *a faith that works*.

The five chapters of the book of James pulsate with life-changing power. Whatever you are going through right now, the book of James has an intensely personal message for you.

Have you lost your job, your business, or your home? Are you struggling in your marriage? Have friends or family members turned against you? Have you lost your reputation? Are you being persecuted for your faith? Then James 1:1-12 is for you.

Do you struggle with temptation in your workplace or on the Internet? Then cling to James 1:13-18. Are you prone to anger? Immerse yourself in James 1:19-21.

Does your faith seem dry, impotent, and unreal? Find the prescription in James 2.

Do your words sometimes get you into trouble or stir up hurt or conflict? Do you have a problem keeping your speech clean? Seek the wisdom of James 3.

Have your thoughts become distorted by the false values of this world? James 4 will straighten out your thinking.

Do you want to understand God's principles for managing money, undergoing suffering, or facing illness? James 5 reveals God's perspective.

The book of James is an intensely practical and realistic book for the age we live in. Technology is constantly changing, but the human condition remains the same. We still sin, suffer, struggle, fight, gossip, grieve, swear, repent, forgive, and pray in the same old ways. And that's why the book of James never goes out of style, never feels out of date. Its message remains as fresh today as when the ink was still wet upon the page.

The book of James is one of the most dynamic and life-changing books in the entire Bible. It is uniquely significant because it was written by the half brother of the Lord Jesus—a man who knew Jesus as no other New Testament writer could.

Matthew 13:55 tells us that the half brothers of Jesus were James, Joseph, Simon, and Judas. And John 7:3-5 tells us that the Lord's brothers did not believe in him. It wasn't until the earthshaking events of the crucifixion and resurrection that James realized that Jesus was the Christ, the Messiah who was promised in the Old Testament.

Though James grew up with Jesus and knew him well in a brotherly way, James never refers to that unique brotherly relationship in this letter. The humility and reverence of James prevents him from mentioning that family connection. Instead, James refers to his half brother as "the Lord Jesus Christ"—a term of awe and devotion. James truly views Jesus not as his big brother but as his Lord and Savior.

As you build these truths from the book of James into your life, you'll discover depths of strength, courage, maturity, and Christian joy you've never known before. So let's turn the page together and plunge into the depths of this amazing document, the book of James.

1

Trials Can Be Your Teacher

No matter who you are and what you might have accomplished in life, when you go back to your hometown, you are still the child the townspeople knew way back when. I found this to be especially true in my life because I was the kid brother in a very large family. It didn't matter to my family that I had ministered all over the world. It didn't matter to the people in my hometown that they had seen me minister to thousands of their friends and neighbors—I was still "that Youssef boy" who used to run around town and stir up trouble.

I came home and I occupied the same position in the family I always had. My family members told me what to eat, what to drink, what to do, where to go, and what mode of transportation to take. I was right back to being the little boy in the family even though I had been married for decades. I was still the little boy who used to get into trouble for fighting with the older siblings. I was still the little boy who got his mouth washed out with soap or got grounded for skipping school.

That experience was an eye-opener. It gave me an entirely new perspective on the author of the epistle of James, the half-brother—the kid brother—of the Lord Jesus.

Can you imagine growing up with Jesus as your big brother? Jesus was perfect! He could *literally* do no wrong. Nothing was ever Jesus's fault. So if something went wrong, if something got broken, if cookies were missing from the cookie jar, James got the blame. He *must* have done it because Jesus certainly wouldn't have.

James undoubtedly saw how different Jesus was from the rest of his siblings—and even from the rest of humanity. You would think that James would have believed in his brother immediately, yet John 7:5 tells us, "For not even his brothers believed in him."

If we had lived in Nazareth at the time James was growing up in the shadow of his big brother, we probably would have seen James complaining to his buddies about Jesus, or making sarcastic remarks about Jesus, or making embarrassed apologies for Jesus. Just as the Old Testament hero Joseph was hated by his brothers and sold into slavery by them, the brothers of Jesus probably found his ideas and actions to be annoying, and at times infuriating. To say that James didn't believe in Jesus might be putting it mildly!

But one day all that changed. A cruel crucifixion silenced Jesus, and he was buried in a grave, sealed up in a tomb. But the grave couldn't contain him; the tomb couldn't hold him. On the third day, Jesus came out of the grave, and for the next forty days, he appeared in person to hundreds and hundreds of eyewitnesses. One of those eyewitnesses was Jesus's kid brother.

The apostle Paul writes of the crucified Lord "that he was buried, that he was raised on the third day in accordance with the Scriptures, and that he appeared to Cephas, then to the twelve. Then he appeared to more than five hundred brothers at one time, most of whom are still alive, though some have fallen asleep. Then he appeared to James, then to all the apostles" (1 Corinthians 15:4-7). The Bible does not disclose any details of that meeting between

James and his risen brother, the Lord Jesus. It doesn't tell us what words were exchanged between them or what memories and emotions they may have shared. We know only this: James was a changed man after that encounter. James was no longer a cynic and a skeptic. He was no longer critical or apologetic about his brother. Paul tells us that James became a "pillar" of the church in Jerusalem (see Galatians 2:9). He was completely sold out—100 percent committed—to Jesus. He gave up everything to follow Jesus. Ultimately, he died following Jesus.

Tradition tells us that James died a martyr's death for the cause of Christ. The Roman-Christian historian and church father Eusebius (c. AD 260–339) gathered the accounts of the death of James from various sources, including *The Antiquities of the Jews* by Josephus, the *Historia Ecclesiae* of Clement of Alexandria, and the now-lost account of Hegesippus in *The Acts of the Church*. According to these records, a group of scribes and Pharisees pushed James from the summit of the temple while he was preaching about Jesus. But the fall didn't kill him. So the religious zealots began to stone him. As they were murdering James, he prayed the same prayer his brother and Lord had prayed on the cross: "Father, forgive them, for they don't know what they are doing." Finally, when James still showed signs of life, one of the men took a staff and delivered a deathblow to the apostle's head.

I'm grateful to God that he inspired James to write the powerful, life-changing letter that bears his name. The epistle of James is written to Christians who are facing tough times, Christians who are facing opposition, hostility, and testing. His purpose in writing this letter was to help all Christians—including you and me—to learn the lessons of their sufferings and to become mature in their faith. James opens his letter with this greeting:

> James, a servant of God and of the Lord Jesus Christ,
>
> To the twelve tribes in the Dispersion:
>
> Greetings (1:1).

The word "servant" in this translation is not strong enough. James uses the Greek word *doulos*, which would be more accurately rendered "bondslave"—a person who is sold into slavery and whose will is not his own. James is not merely calling himself a servant, such as a butler or maid, who is free to resign and seek other employment. He is a bondslave, a slave in chains, a person whose will is surrendered, who lives solely for the cause of Christ, his Master. These opening lines are the letterhead of the epistle of James. If I were to write a letter, I would send that letter out on the letterhead of The Church of The Apostles, a sheet of paper imprinted with the logo of our church. James too has a letterhead and a logo. His letterhead is James 1:1, and his logo is the word *bondslave*. That's the title, credential, and official seal of the apostle James. He confesses publicly, at the beginning of his letter, that he is the property of another. His life and his will are not his own.

You might think he would introduce himself as "a servant of God and *the brother* of the Lord Jesus Christ." Wouldn't that be a great way to make an impression on new believers? Wouldn't that be an impressive credential to display? But James doesn't mention his genetic relationship to Jesus through their mother, Mary. The only relationship he claims in his opening lines is the relationship of a bondslave, an abject servant of Jesus the Master.

In those days, just as in our own time, people were impressed by your family connections. People were impressed by *who* you knew more than what you knew. James could have easily exploited his family relationship with Jesus. He could have even rationalized, "I'm not doing this to inflate my own ego. I just want to impress audiences so I can share the gospel." But James wasn't trying to impress anyone. He simply wanted to be known as a bondslave of Jesus.

If I were writing this epistle, and I wanted to get the undivided attention of my readers, I think I would have milked my half-brother relationship with Jesus to the fullest! I would have written, "Please be advised that I am the Right Reverend Bishop James of Jerusalem, a chosen Apostle and the Half-Brother (on our Mother's side) of the Lord Jesus, who is the Christ and the Only Begotten Son of the Father."

Now, that's a set of credentials! That would establish me as an SVIP—a Spiritually Very Important Person. No one would ever ask, "James who?" In fact, I would probably have my family tree printed on a T-shirt so I could wear it all the time.

But James does not want to seek prominence for himself. He wants to lift up and glorify Jesus. That's why he refers to Jesus by his full title, "the Lord Jesus Christ." He is the Lord, the Ruler and Master. He is Jesus, the Savior; his name means "God (Yahweh) saves." And he is the Christ (*Christos*), which is the Greek form of the word *Messiah*—"the anointed one."

James calls himself a bondslave of the Lord Jesus Christ. What does he mean? He is saying, "I do the will of the Master. I obey his will, not my own. I give total control of my life to the Master. That is my identity. That is who I am—a bondslave, a man with no will but to obey the will of the Master." A slave is not permitted to have a divided allegiance. He cannot serve the Master while looking out for his own interests. A slave has no will of his own.

It's significant that James, the half-brother of Jesus, affirms the divinity of the Lord Jesus Christ. Think about what this means. No one knows your weaknesses and shortcomings better than a member of your family. If Jesus had ever lied, cheated, cursed, gotten even, brawled, or behaved in a petty or jealous way, James would have known. Brothers always know.

Yet James recognized that his half-brother was nothing less than God in human flesh. I can't imagine a more reliable and credible testimony than this!

Unfluttered hearts and unshaken faith

After the brief "letterhead" greeting, James leaps right into one of his key themes in this letter—the theme that trials and sufferings

can be a great teacher, producing growth and character strength in
our lives:

> Count it all joy, my brothers, when you meet trials of
> various kinds, for you know that the testing of your faith
> produces steadfastness (1:2-3).

How do you respond when you face intense hurts, disappoint-
ments, setbacks, and sorrows? How do you respond when the walls
close in? James tells us what a spiritually healthy and godly response
looks like. For many of us, these verses are an unpleasant medicine,
hard to swallow, difficult to accept. But the truth of this principle
is undeniable: trials and sufferings often have a purpose in our lives.
Trials have a way of nudging unbelievers toward God and helping
believers to grow stronger and more mature in the faith.

Someone asked Christian philosopher C.S. Lewis, "Why do
righteous people suffer?" Lewis replied, "Why shouldn't the righteous suffer? They're the only ones who can take it."

We tend to fear trials as if they are the undertaker. But the truth
is that trials, viewed from a godly and spiritual perspective, can truly
be our teachers to make us wiser and stronger. Notice that James
doesn't tell us to merely put up with our trials. He doesn't tell us to
endure our trials without complaining. He tells us to "count it all
joy," to consider it a *good* thing when we encounter various trials.
And he doesn't say *if* we face trials, but *when* we face trials. In this
life, suffering and sorrow are inevitable, but God wants us to face
our trials with an attitude of joy.

In many corners of the church today, we see presentations of
a "happy talk" gospel, a version of the Christian faith that is nothing more than adding the name of Jesus to your Sunday vocabulary,
adding Sunday morning to your busy schedule, and adding a few
dollars a year to the collection plate. In this version of Christianity, God does not demand that we change our behavior, change our
thinking, or change our ethical and moral standards.

The pale pastel Christianity that is so often declared today would have been unrecognizable to Christians in the first century. James wrote his epistle to Christians who were being persecuted, imprisoned, tortured, and killed for simply believing and saying that Jesus is Lord. In the face of all the suffering the early Christians endured, the message of James was, "You must consider all your sufferings as joy."

Joy? What does that mean? How can we consider our sufferings as joy? What was James suggesting? Is the apostle saying that we should paste a Cheshire cat smile on our faces and put on a brave spiritual front while holding back our tears? Was he suggesting that we should be phony and insincere about our hurts and our emotions?

Was James saying we should say, "Oh, how wonderful, I lost my job!"? Or "This heart attack is such a blessing in my life—it makes me so happy!"? No! Please understand—God does not want us to display hypocritical happy faces. He doesn't want us to hide our hurts behind a happy Christian mask. Nor does he want churches filled with grim, iron-willed stoics who deny their feelings, who reject their emotions, who pretend their heartbreaks never happened.

But God wants us to reach a place in our walk with him where we can face trials and tragedies with unfluttered hearts and unshaken faith. He wants us to know peace in the midst of upheaval and uncertainty. He wants us to experience the peace that surpasses understanding, a godly contentment and honest submission to the Father's plan.

I often talk to Christians who are going through a time of suffering, setback, or opposition, and they tell me they feel God has abandoned them. They assume that Satan has the upper hand. It's understandable that people sometimes cry out in confusion because of their pain—but God wants us to reach a place of spiritual maturity where we trust his goodness, his wisdom, and his love in spite of our suffering and pain.

Yes, Satan is the god of this world—but Satan does not have the upper hand in our lives. The power of Satan does not trump the power of God. To ascribe power to Satan in our times of adversity is to deny God's sovereignty over our lives and over the world. Satan operates within the systems of this world, and he has certain freedoms for a limited period of time. *But Satan is under the power and sovereign authority of God.* He cannot do anything unless God allows it.

So we have to ask ourselves: Why does God allow believers to suffer? Isn't he able to prevent our suffering? Doesn't he want to stop our suffering? Why do bad things happen to God's people?

The ultimate answer is that God knows what he is doing. Our sovereign God knows what we need so that we will grow to be mature in Jesus Christ. Trials that seem to invade our lives, trials that are beyond our control, don't happen because God is unhappy with us. Trials do sometimes come to us in the form of discipline, designed to lead us away from sin and back to God, as the Scriptures teach us: "It is for discipline that you have to endure. God is treating you as sons. For what son is there whom his father does not discipline?" (Hebrews 12:7).

The moment we face a crisis in our lives, we go crying out to God, "Lord, please change this crisis! Lord, please change these circumstances!" We rarely stop and ask ourselves: "What if God wants to change *me*?"

Facing a marital crisis, we are quick to say, "Lord, please change my wife," or "Please change my husband." In reality, God probably wants to change us.

In a financial crisis, we are quick to say, "Lord, please send money!" or "Please save my business!" In reality, God probably wants to change us.

Facing a health crisis and a frightening diagnosis, we are quick to say, "Lord, please heal my body," or "Please remove this illness," or "Please let the test results be a mistake." But what if God wants to heal our soul, our spirit, and our relationship with him instead? What if he wants to use your sufferings to make you more like his Son, Jesus Christ?

You might say, "God, if you would change my boss, my job would be perfect!" But God may have placed that boss in your path to teach you something about the Christian life. You might say, "God, if you would change my atheist professor so that he'd stop mocking my faith, I would have a great experience in college." But God probably placed that professor in your path to teach you how to stand firm for Christ in the face of persecution.

God is constantly teaching us lessons through our daily experiences. He wants us to become spiritually mature. He wants us to master today's challenges, and he wants to equip us to take on even greater challenges tomorrow. As George MacDonald, that great nineteenth-century Scottish pastor and author, once observed, "The Son of God…suffered unto the death, not that we might not suffer, but that our sufferings might be like his."[2]

Trials 101

Jesus said that trees need to be pruned in order to bear fruit: "Every branch that does bear fruit he [God the Father] prunes, that it may bear more fruit" (John 15:2). Pruning a tree is a process of cutting away branches, buds, and deadwood in order to improve the health and productivity of a fruit tree or vine. Every gardener worth his green thumb will tell you that Jesus is giving sound horticultural advice as well as sound spiritual advice.

When a believer gets his or her branch nipped through trials and suffering, it hurts. But it also causes us to bear fruit and have joy in the midst of the trials, because each trouble, each heartache, is designed by the Father to prune us, to improve our spiritual health, and to make us more productive for God.

James wants us to think of the Christian life as a college course called Trials 101. It's part of the divine curriculum for every believer.

We are students in the School of Hard Knocks, and trials serve as our teacher.

Malcolm Muggeridge was the longtime editor of Britain's popular *Punch* magazine and a cynic and atheist for most of his life. He converted to Christ late in life and became a strong, influential witness for Christ. In a book called *A Twentieth Century Testimony*, he wrote, "I can say with complete truthfulness that everything I have learned in my seventy-five years in this world, everything that has truly enhanced and enlightened my experience, has been through affliction and not through happiness...This, of course, is what the cross signifies. And it is the cross, more than anything else, that has called me inexorably to Christ."[3]

You might say, "Well, my life has been going pretty well. I really don't have any trials to speak of." Look out, my friend, because you are still being tested. There are four stages that every believer goes through:

- *Stage 1: Faith.* You come to Christ and you trust in God. You begin living the Christian life as you believe in his Word.

- *Stage 2: Obedience.* As your Christian experience deepens and God's Word takes root in your life, you begin to obey God more intensely, you take his Word more seriously, and your growing obedience proves that your faith is genuine.

- *Stage 3: Blessing.* God blesses your obedience. You rejoice in him, and everything seems to be going well. Then comes the next stage.

- *Stage 4: Testing.* Blessings always lead to testing.

God permits our faith to be tested for at least three reasons: First, we are tested to prove whether our faith is genuine. Second, we are tested so that our faith will grow and become more mature. Third, we are tested in order to bring glory to the Lord.

The very blessings God brings into our lives are a test. God wants to reveal the reality of our faith and character. The test of blessing will reveal: whether our blessings cause us to let go of faith and begin living by sight; whether our blessings cause us to focus on the blessings and forget the Blesser; and whether our blessings increase our smugness and self-pride or increase our dependence upon God.

As the Scottish Christian essayist Thomas Carlyle once observed, "Adversity is sometimes hard upon a man; but for one man who can stand prosperity, there are a hundred that will stand adversity."

God's wisdom for trying times

What is our responsibility in the process of trial and testing? James goes on to tell us:

> And let steadfastness have its full effect, that you may be perfect and complete, lacking in nothing (1:4).

James is saying: Don't fight God's perfect work in your life. Don't rebel against the circumstances he has allowed in your life. Instead, allow the testing process to go on to completion so that you may receive the maximum benefit of God's teaching and maturing ministry. Allow God to work through the circumstances and challenges of your life. If you rebel against your circumstances, if all you want is to escape your trials and problems, you will never become mature in Christ.

How, then, should we respond to our trials? James goes on to tell us:

> If any of you lacks wisdom, let him ask God, who gives generously to all without reproach, and it will be given him (1:5).

Imagine this scenario with me: You possess a piece of paper with a secret code written on it. You can use that secret code to open a safe. Inside that safe are all the resources you need to empower you and strengthen you to live the Christian life—resources beyond your imagination. What are those resources? They are the insight, understanding, judgment, and discernment that, collectively, are known as the wisdom of God.

The Lord's wisdom is the greatest resource available to you for your spiritual growth. The wisdom of God enables us to know what God plans to accomplish in our lives. His wisdom is the defogger for the clouded lenses of our human understanding. When we ask God for his wisdom, we open ourselves up to learn about life from God's perspective.

Why do so many Christians remain immature in their character and stagnant in their faith? It's because they are unable to see life from God's panoramic perspective. They remain mired in their limited human perspective, so they are never able to see past their circumstances and sufferings. When trials come, immature Christians say, "God, get me out of this mess!"

Godly, mature Christians look at their trials and say, "God, I don't understand why this is happening to me. I need more of your wisdom. Please make me wise to understand my problems from your perspective. I don't expect you to lift me out of my trials, but I ask you to lead me safely and wisely through my trials, so that I can give all the glory to you."

That's God's wisdom talking. Wisdom is God's wide-angle lens on the problems and trials of this life, but wisdom doesn't fall on us like rain from the sky. We have to ask God for his wisdom. When we ask for wisdom, he will give it to us, generously and without reproach. That is God's promise to us in James 1:5.

How do you ask for wisdom in the midst of challenging circumstances? James goes on to give us the answer:

> But let him ask in faith, with no doubting, for the one who doubts is like a wave of the sea that is driven and tossed by the wind. For that person must not suppose that he will receive anything from the Lord; he is a double-minded man, unstable in all his ways (1:6-8).

The person who asks for wisdom while doubting God is vacillating between trust and trying to go it alone. That person is hesitant and uncertain about God's love, power, and wisdom. Such people cannot expect to receive wisdom from the Lord. Godly wisdom comes only when we are fully, genuinely, completely, seriously (and any other superlative you can think of) trusting in God.

Don't expect God to be honored by a half-hearted commitment or a part-time allegiance. He is not pleased when we trust him one moment and doubt him the next.

The victory is already ours

James goes on to tell us that trials are a great leveler of the human race:

> Let the lowly brother boast in his exaltation, and the rich in his humiliation, because like a flower of the grass he will pass away. For the sun rises with its scorching heat and withers the grass; its flower falls, and its beauty perishes. So also will the rich man fade away in the midst of his pursuits (1:9-11).

The rich pass through trials. So do the poor. Illness shows no partiality. Death does not discriminate. When a godly Christian suffers, whether he is rich or poor, he must cling to the promises of God. The poor are exalted by the riches of God's grace. The rich are humbled by the fact that they are like the flower of the grass, which passes away. The most exalted earthly title means absolutely nothing compared with the privilege of being a bondslave to Christ.

Earthly possessions have a way of clouding eternal issues and interfering with our fellowship with God. Possessions demand our attention. They claim our affection. And when trials come, those who have great earthly possessions often find their lives complicated. Possessions can be a snare.

We worry about losing the things we have accumulated. Have

we protected our possessions from fire? Flood? Theft? Inflation? Recession? Depression? In challenging times, it's easy to become so focused on our material goals that we forget our spiritual priorities. That is why James warns that, in times of trial, the rich should glory in their humiliation. They should glory in the fact that they can depend on the loving Father. Even if their bank accounts were to evaporate, God will still be there to lean on.

Material possessions are fleeting. Only a relationship with God through Jesus Christ endures throughout eternity. That is the vital, sustaining relationship you can rely on, that you can count on, no matter what setbacks and losses you suffer in this life.

What is our reason for considering it all joy when we suffer trials? James tells us:

> Blessed is the man who remains steadfast under trial, for when he has stood the test he will receive the crown of life, which God has promised to those who love him (1:12).

We rejoice because of the victory that is already ours in Christ. Jesus has already won the victory, and God has promised the crown of victory to all those who love him. We can experience joy in our trials if we trust God to use those trials to bring forth Christlike character and growth in us.

In the early church, no one expected a life of ease, good health, and prosperity, as so many Christians expect today. The late preacher Vance Havner observed that more than three hundred delegates attended the First Nicene Council in AD 325. Out of all the delegates who came to Nicaea (in modern Turkey) from around the ancient world, fewer than a dozen were completely whole in body. All the rest had been tortured and mutilated for their faith, losing an eye or limb or hand because they refused to stop preaching the gospel of Jesus Christ. If you are obedient to Christ, you will be at war with this world—and the world will make you suffer for it.[4]

Trials can be our teacher, because God can use the worst that happens to us to build his best within us. When trials come, we can choose resentment and bitterness over the "unfairness" of life's trials—or we can learn the eternal lessons God wants to teach us. Which will you choose?

2

Giving In to Temptation

Marathon runners tell me there comes a point during the marathon known as "hitting the wall." This is the worst part of the run—a barrier of pain and exhaustion. Your muscles cramp. Your body screams at you. Physically and mentally, you want to quit in the worst way. When a runner "hits the wall," he or she has a choice: either surrender to the temptation to quit or keep running right through the wall.

In the next section of James 1, the apostle tells us how Christians spiritually hit the wall. This is a normal part of the Christian life, and James tells us how to respond when we experience it. He tells us that those who choose to quit and drop out of the race will simply stunt their spiritual growth. Those who persevere and push through the wall will experience renewed vigor and growth in their Christian life.

Every day, Christians hit the wall and face a crucial decision. Every day, Satan's weapons are aimed at the hearts of believers. Every day, Christians are tempted to quit. The growing, healthy Christian is the one who refuses to lower his shield. He refuses to surrender to sin. He refuses to surrender to spiritual paralysis. He refuses to surrender to spiritual exhaustion and spiritual pain. He perseveres. He pushes through the wall and presses on toward the prize.

We have all known this temptation from our earliest Christian experience, even from childhood. Children face that temptation regularly. Faced with the temptation to confess their sin or deny it, children will often say, "It wasn't my fault. The devil made me do it."

I once heard about a mother who told her young son, "I'm going next door for just a few minutes. While I'm gone, do not get into the jar of jam!"

"I won't," the little boy said.

When the mother returned, she found her son with jam on his shirt, his fingers, and around his mouth. She said, "Didn't I tell you not to get into the jam?"

"Yes, Momma, you did."

"And haven't I told you that when Satan tempts you to disobey, you should tell him to get behind you?"

"Yes, Momma," the boy said, "but when he got behind me, he pushed me right to the jam jar!"

Adults use the same flimsy excuse all the time. It's a behavior pattern that goes back to Adam and Eve. After the first man and woman yielded to Satan's temptation and ate of the forbidden fruit, God confronted Adam, saying, "Have you eaten of the tree of which I commanded you not to eat?" Adam replied, "*The woman whom you gave to be with me*, she gave me fruit of the tree, and I ate." In one neat turn of phrase, Adam shifted the blame not only to Eve but to God, who gave Eve to Adam. When God confronted the woman, she said, "The serpent deceived me, and I ate" (Genesis 3:11-13). In other words, "The devil made me do it."

Adam and Eve were given a beautiful garden, the freedom to roam anywhere in the garden and enjoy its bounty, the privilege of direct fellowship with God. But instead of saying no to the devil, they yielded to temptation—and when confronted with their spiritual and moral failure, they said, "God, it's your fault."

And that has been the dysfunctional human response to sin, shame, and guilt ever since. We say, "It's not my fault! Don't blame me! It's my wife's fault, my husband's fault, the boss's fault, the neighbor's fault, society's fault, the devil's fault. My kids drove me crazy, and I just couldn't help myself. I needed the money, or I was tempted by a sexual opportunity, or I was tempted by loneliness and boredom—and anyone in my situation would have done the same thing. And actually, God, you deserve most of the blame because you allowed me to be in that situation. You created me with urges and weaknesses. You allowed me to be tempted! You gave me free will! It's your fault that I failed."

On the other hand, some people beat themselves to death with guilt—both real guilt and false guilt. Let me give you a few examples of false guilt.

Many parents who have done all they could to raise healthy, responsible, godly children feel guilty when a child grows up to become a dysfunctional, irresponsible, godless adult. Some parents blame themselves, despite the fact that children have free will and have rebelled against godly teaching. That is frequently false guilt.

Physically or sexually abused kids often grow up with self-hate, self-blame, and false guilt over their abuse, even though it is the abuser who deserves all the guilt. In fact, sexual predators commonly use false guilt to manipulate, control, and silence their victims. Abused kids are victims, and any guilt they suffer for the abuse is false guilt.

Abused wives often take the abuser's guilt onto themselves, saying, "It wasn't my husband's fault. It was my fault for serving dinner late and leaving the house in a mess. He had a right to be angry." That is false guilt. A man who uses violence against his wife is completely without excuse.

Whether the guilt feelings you suffer are deserved or undeserved, authentic or false, guilt is a spiritual sickness. God wants to deliver you from the fear, shame, and guilt of the spiritual sickness that comes from sin. The Scriptures do not teach us that we should remain mired in either authentic guilt or false guilt. From Genesis to Revelation, and especially here in James 1, God tells us he has delivered us from the oppressive weight of guilt and sin.

Where does temptation come from?

James tells us, first of all, that temptation does not begin with God or come from God. Where, then, does temptation come from? James writes:

> Let no one say when he is tempted, "I am being tempted by God," for God cannot be tempted with evil, and he himself tempts no one. But each person is tempted when he is lured and enticed by his own desire. Then desire when it has conceived gives birth to sin, and sin when it is fully grown brings forth death (1:13-15).

God does not tempt us. We are tempted by our own desires that well up within us and ultimately become uncontrollable and destructive, like a river overflowing its banks. An uncontrolled desire, like a river at flood stage, turns a blessing into a curse, a pleasurable urge into a destructive force. From the dawn of time, temptation has been a strategy of the evil one. Just as he did with Adam and Eve, Satan uses our eyes, our minds, and our internal desires to ruin our loving, obedient relationship with God.

Eve's excuse for her sin was, "The serpent deceived me, and I ate." The flimsiness of this excuse is instantly obvious: her big mistake was talking to serpents! She flirted with temptation. She placed herself in a dangerous position, where Satan could plant doubts in her mind about God's goodness, while stirring up a desire for the attractive but forbidden fruit.

Satan always attacks us with a double-barreled shotgun. One barrel is the mind; the other barrel is the eye. Satan came to Eve and began playing with her mind: "Eve, you've got it made, girl! What a beautiful garden! I wish I could live like you. This is fantastic." Then he attacked her through the pleasures of the eye: "Just look at all those beautiful trees! And I hear there's a special tree in the middle of the garden. Its fruit tastes incredible!"

When Eve replies that the fruit of that tree is forbidden by God, Satan goes back to playing mind games on her: "Forbidden? Really? Well, I suppose God knows something he doesn't want you to know. If you ate from that tree, your eyes would be opened and you'd be just like God. What a selfish God he must be to forbid you to eat the most incredible fruit in the garden. Too bad he wants to keep all the good stuff for himself."

The tempter attacked Eve through the mind and the eyes—and she fell for it hook, line, and sinker. She probably never gave the forbidden tree much thought at first, but once those doubts were planted in her mind, she couldn't pass the tree without pondering Satan's sly words. Like a good fisherman, Satan lured Eve, then hooked her, and finally he reeled her in. And the rest is history— thousands of years of tragic, sin-riddled human history.

It's important to understand that Satan didn't *force* Eve to eat the forbidden fruit. He could lure her and tempt her and worm his way into her thoughts, but Eve always had free will. Satan couldn't make the choice for her. She made that choice herself.

We like to pretend that, when tempted, we have no choice but to give in. We claim we simply couldn't help ourselves. But the real problem with temptation is not that we have no choice, but that *we make the choices* that lead to temptation. Once we make the choice to live dangerously and flirt with temptation, we have already placed our feet on the path to sin.

One way to safeguard ourselves against temptation is to remember the Lord's Prayer. Did you know that 20 percent of this prayer deals with temptation? In Matthew 6:13, Jesus teaches us to pray, "And lead us not into temptation, but deliver us from evil."

What if we would memorize that verse and pray that prayer every time we are tempted to sin? What if we posted Matthew 6:13 on the refrigerator door as a reminder not to yield to gluttony; on the dashboard of the car to remind us to obey the speed laws and to be courteous to other drivers; on our computer desktop to remind us to avoid sinful websites; on the cell phone to remind us to speak only words that are edifying and uplifting. What if you met every temptation in your life with, "Lord, lead me not into temptation, but deliver me from evil." How might your life be transformed by that prayer?

Satan can't force any believer to do anything against his or her will. The devil can't make you do anything. If you yield to temptation, you have no one to blame but yourself. We can kid ourselves all we want, pretending that "the devil made me do it," but the truth is that we will never experience growth, maturity, and Christlikeness until we deal with temptation and sin in our lives.

Garbage in, garbage out

On the last Saturday morning of January 1999, Eugene Robinson, a defensive player for the Atlanta Falcons, received the Bart Starr Award for high moral character. Nicknamed "Prophet," Robinson was widely known for his strong Christian witness and his devotion to his family. The following day he would be playing in the most important game of his career, Super Bowl XXXIII.

But that very night, Robinson was arrested by an undercover police officer and charged with soliciting for prostitution. He was booked and released, and then returned to his hotel. But Robinson was unable to sleep that night.

The media was quick to trash him as a hypocrite. In the Super Bowl, he appeared distracted and off his rhythm. By the end of the game, the Falcons had lost to the Denver Broncos, 34 to 19.

After the game, Robinson held a press conference and told reporters, "I apologize to my Lord Jesus Christ, to my wife and kids, and to the NFL family for the distraction this has caused. Confession is good for the soul, but bad for the reputation. I truly love my wife and kids, and I regret that this has hurt them." He later returned the Bart Starr Award.

Despite his nickname, Eugene Robinson was not a prophet. He was just a man who caved in to temptation.

You and I are no different from him, except that our failures are usually not played out before a national TV audience. We all have this war going on within us. Our enemy knows our vulnerabilities and will exploit them any way he can in order to destroy us and discredit our witness.

If you are a follower of Christ, but you have lost some battles against temptation, then I have good news for you: God has made it possible for you to get back on track. He does not change his mind about your salvation every time you fail. He doesn't rewrite his will each time you stumble and disobey. As the Lord Jesus said:

> "My sheep hear my voice, and I know them, and they follow me. I give them eternal life, and they will never perish, and no one will snatch them out of my hand. My Father, who has given them to me, is greater than all, and no one is able to snatch them out of the Father's hand" (John 10:27-29).

Satan tempts us in three principle ways.

First, he will often tempt us *spiritually*. He will bring doubts into our minds: Is God real? Does he exist? Is there really life after death? Is the Bible true? Does God really love me? Are my sins really forgiven? Satan often sends these questions into our minds to make us doubt God and doubt the reality of our relationship with him.

Second, Satan will tempt us *mentally*. This form of temptation often comes from the culture around us. When we grow careless about what we read and watch in movies or television, we set ourselves up for this form of temptation. It's the GIGO principle that computer programmers have long known about—"garbage in, garbage out." If you put faulty information into a computer, you are going to get faulty results. If you fill your mind with bad information, false beliefs, and sinful images, then the things you think, say, and do are going to be defiled and corrupted.

The battle for your mind begins the moment you wake up. How do you start your day? With the morning news? While it's good to be informed about the world, opening your day with bad news is a sure way to get depressed. Should you start the day by thinking of all the tasks you have to complete that day? Well, that's a sure way to become overwhelmed and discouraged.

I suggest a different course of action. As soon as I'm awake each day, even before I get out of bed, I begin talking to God. I don't waste any time, I just begin talking to the Lord. I thank him for the new day and for the rest I received through the night (even if it was only two or three hours). Then I offer my body as a living sacrifice to him, asking him to use me as he chooses in order to accomplish his purpose through my life.

Try it for a few weeks. I think you'll find that the awareness of God's presence each morning will tend to stay with you throughout the day.

Third, we are tempted *physically*. How does Satan tempt us physically? Let me count the ways! You may experience frustration or anger over a car that won't start, plumbing that plugs up, a driver who cuts you off on the freeway, an obnoxious boss or coworker, or some other frustrating event—so you cuss and you swear and you sin with your tongue. Or you might be lured into abusing drugs or alcohol—and one day you realize you are an addict. Or you see an opportunity to cheat a client or cheat your boss or cheat on your taxes—and though you know it is a sin, you rationalize your guilt and say, "Everybody cheats to get ahead."

One of the most common physical temptations occurs when you notice an attractive person of the opposite sex and momentarily forget your wedding vows. I once heard about a husband who accompanied his wife on a trip to the department store. While the wife examined items on a sale table, an attractive young woman walked by. The husband, thinking his wife was too busy to notice, followed the young woman with his eyes. The wife apparently had eyes in the back of her head, because without even looking up from the sale table, she asked, "Was it worth the trouble you're in?"

How quickly we set aside our Christian convictions when the allure of temptation comes our way. While it's true that God has given our bodies natural desires, these desires are to be used within healthy and godly boundaries. If the desire is of a sexual nature, the boundaries are those of a marriage relationship between a husband and wife. This means that sexual expression outside of that marriage relationship is sin. That's why adultery is sin, fornication is sin, and homosexuality is sin.

Tested or tempted?

People sometimes ask me, "What is the difference between testing and tempting?" The answer to that question is simple. We enjoy temptation. We hate testing. Temptation involves pleasure. Testing involves unpleasantness. Temptation is easy. Tests are hard.

In a time of testing, God identifies a problem area in your life and says, "This must go. This must change." Through that test, a mature Christian is able to learn and grow. A test says, "Learn the lessons of this test. Become more responsible and more mature in Christ." But temptation says, "Give in. Yield. Surrender. It would be so easy to simply say yes to temptation, and all of these pleasures will be yours."

Testing says, "Sacrifice your desires." Temptation says, "Satisfy your desires."

When you submit to spiritual testing, you grow strong and mature in the Christian life. When you surrender to temptation, you remain a spiritual infant—childish and undisciplined, a slave to your desires, easily manipulated by Satan. James put his finger on the difference between testing and temptation in verse 13: "Let no one say when he is tempted, 'I am being tempted by God,' for God cannot be tempted with evil, and he himself tempts no one."

That was Adam's error when he blamed his sin on "the *woman* whom *you* gave to be with me," blaming both Eve and God in the same breath. And it's the same error you and I easily fall into when we are tempted—the error of blaming others, blaming circumstances, blaming society, and blaming God for the choices we make of our own free will. And many Christians, when they fail to understand the difference between testing and temptation, sometimes succumb to temptation and reap the bitter consequences—and then they blame God for "testing" them with temptation. Blaming God for our temptations, James says, is something we must not do.

Unfortunately, generations of people have grown up being told they are not to blame for anything that is wrong with their lives. They are told it was bad parenting or inadequate education or social injustice that caused their dysfunctional behavior. And many Christians have bought into the don't-blame-me mentality. So when Christians yield to temptation and suffer the consequences of sin, they often shift the blame instead of following the biblical prescription.

And what does the Bible prescribe whenever we suffer the consequences of sin? "If we say we have no sin, we deceive ourselves, and the truth is not in us. If we confess our sins, he is faithful and just to forgive us our sins and to cleanse us from all unrighteousness" (1 John 1:8-9). Instead of shifting the blame and saying we have no sin, we have to acknowledge and admit our sin. Once we confess our sin, claiming nothing but the righteousness of Christ, God will forgive our sin and make us clean.

In order to be cleansed of guilt, we must first accept and acknowledge our guilt. As long as we deny our guilt and shift the blame, God cannot cleanse us. We must confess and judge the sin in our lives, repent of it and deal with it, asking God for the power to flee temptation in the future.

Yes, it's true that Satan does attack us. He has attacked us in the past, he will attack us in the future, he will always attack us. But the attacks of Satan do not relieve us of responsibility to flee temptation. As the apostle Paul wrote to the believers in Corinth, "No temptation has overtaken you that is not common to man. God is faithful, and he will not let you be tempted beyond your ability, but with the temptation he will also provide the way of escape, that you may be able to endure it" (1 Corinthians 10:13).

If you are under attack, then flee your attacker, run for cover, shield yourself! If someone is shooting at you, it would be insane to walk right into the hail of bullets. Yet that's exactly how many people respond to the attacks of Satan. Instead of fleeing temptation, they move toward it and discuss terms of surrender. Once you begin to negotiate your surrender with Satan, he has already conquered you. That is why the Bible says, again and again, that we must flee temptation (see 1 Corinthians 6:18; 1 Corinthians 10:14; 1 Timothy 6:11; 2 Timothy 2:22).

Consider the Old Testament hero Joseph. In many ways, Joseph is an Old Testament symbol of Jesus. Loved by his father, hated by his brothers, Joseph was betrayed and sold into slavery for twenty pieces of silver. He became a suffering servant and was later exalted to kingly power in Egypt as Pharaoh's right-hand man.

One of the key incidents in the story of Joseph takes place in Genesis 39. There, an Egyptian army captain named Potiphar buys Joseph from the slave merchants. As Potiphar's slave, Joseph demonstrates strong character, integrity, responsibility, and leadership. Potiphar soon entrusts Joseph—a mere teenager—with his entire household, finances, and possessions.

But Potiphar's wife is an unfaithful seductress. She approaches Joseph—not once but again and again, day after day (see Genesis 39:10). But Joseph will not compromise his integrity, even under constant, daily temptation. He refuses to sin against Potiphar—and against God. Even though the barrage of temptation is daily and inescapable, Joseph refuses to give in because to do so would mean betraying his relationship with God.

How is Joseph rewarded for his faith and integrity? Potiphar's wife becomes enraged, and she lies about Joseph to her husband, claiming Joseph tried to rape her. So Potiphar sends Joseph to prison. There is often a price to pay for following God and fleeing temptation, but God expects us to willingly pay that price.

Giving in to temptation is easy. Fleeing temptation is hard. Though our salvation is a free gift of God's grace, the cost of following Christ every day is high. As Jesus himself said, "If anyone would come after me, let him deny himself and take up his cross daily and follow me" (Luke 9:23).

The greatest gift of all

What makes us vulnerable to temptation? Why do even Christians find themselves enslaved by the pursuit of pleasure, the lure of unchecked desire, and the attraction of unrestrained lusts? James tells us it is because we are unwilling to tap into the limitless power of the Holy Spirit. He writes:

> Do not be deceived, my beloved brothers. Every good gift and every perfect gift is from above, coming down from the Father of lights with whom there is no variation or shadow due to change. Of his own will he brought us forth by the word of truth, that we should be a kind of firstfruits of his creatures (1:16-18).

James tells us that not only is God *not* the one who tempts us, he is actually the Giver of all good gifts. Among these is the gift of the Holy Spirit.

That great evangelist of a previous era, Dwight L. Moody, had a great way of illustrating how the Holy Spirit can help us overcome temptation. He would set an empty drinking glass on a table and say to his audience, "How can I take the air out of this glass?"

Someone in the audience might say, "Pump the air out of the glass with a pump."

"If you did that," Moody would reply, "you'd create a vacuum inside the glass—and the air pressure outside the glass would shatter it."

When no one in the audience could figure out how to take the air out of the glass, Moody would take a pitcher of water and fill the glass to the brim. Then he'd say, "You see? All the air has been removed from the glass. If you want to empty a vessel of one substance, fill it completely with another substance. In the same way, if you want to remove all the sin from your life, fill your life completely with the Holy Spirit."

The filling of the Spirit is the secret to escaping the temptation of Satan. The filling of the Spirit replaces our old human sin nature with the new godly nature of God himself. As long as the Spirit fills you, temptation has no power over you. But the moment you grieve the Holy Spirit, Satan has access to your soul. When you quench the Spirit by silencing his voice, you make yourself vulnerable to temptation.

Temptation and sin are far more serious than most of us suppose. Christians who habitually yield to temptation bring serious spiritual, emotional, and even physical harm upon themselves. God sometimes allows those who habitually sin to undergo physical death—not as a punishment but as an act of mercy. It is far more merciful for God to take a habitually sinning believer home than to allow that person to go on harming himself and others with his pattern of sin. We see this principle in the church at Corinth where, Paul tells us, some Christians died because of their habitual sins (see 1 Corinthians 5:5 and 11:30). Persistent, habitual sin can also bring other consequences on us as believers—broken marriages, harm to children, disease, damaged friendships, addiction, financial problems, shame and guilt, ruined reputations, and more. God does not tempt us. He is the Giver of all good gifts. He gives us the Holy Spirit and the power to flee temptation and experience victory over sin. He gives us reason to praise and thank him. Jesus is more than adequate to meet all your needs, to give you strength when you are weak, to give you the power to say no, even to daily, relentless temptation. Call on him, and he will answer. Pray to him, and he will bless you. And the greatest gift and blessing of all is the Holy Spirit, who gives us the power to flee temptation.

3

You Can't Grow Without the Word

B eing slow to listen can be fatal.

The Battle of Little Bighorn—often called "Custer's Last Stand"—came after a lengthy history of conflict between the United States government and the Native American tribes. For years, the government had repeatedly broken treaties with the tribes. The long conflict culminated in the infamous battle between General George Armstrong Custer's Seventh Cavalry and the combined forces of the Lakota Sioux, Arapaho, and Northern Cheyenne tribes.

History remembers Custer as a supremely confident man who did not listen well. When the army offered him an additional battalion of soldiers and a battery of Gatling guns, Custer refused, boasting that his Seventh Cavalry could handle any threat. He didn't listen to his superiors. When his Indian scouts warned him that he should not spread his forces too thin, Custer ignored them. He didn't listen to his scouts. When the Native American tribes repeatedly begged Custer to obey the treaties so war could be averted, Custer refused to listen to them.

So, on June 26, 1876, Custer led a force of seven hundred mounted soldiers along the Little Bighorn River in eastern Montana Territory. Some eighteen hundred Native American warriors were waiting for him. The result: slaughter and defeat for the United States Army. Custer was shot in the head and chest, and he died on the battlefield.

Following the battle, two Cheyenne women went out on the corpse-strewn battlefield and found a group of warriors huddled around Custer's lifeless body. The warriors were preparing to take revenge on Custer by desecrating his body. The Cheyenne women shooed the warriors off. Then they took awls and pushed them deep into Custer's ears. They did so not to desecrate his body, but as an act of mercy toward his spirit. They believed that the holes in Custer's ears might help him listen better in the afterlife.[5]

James too wants us to become better listeners. Above all, he wants us to listen to the Word of truth. So in this section of his epistle, James writes:

> Know this, my beloved brothers: let every person be
> quick to hear, slow to speak, slow to anger; for the anger
> of man does not produce the righteousness of God.
> Therefore put away all filthiness and rampant wicked-
> ness and receive with meekness the implanted word,
> which is able to save your souls (1:19-21).

In these verses, James describes for us the behavior that the Word of God produces in the life of a believer. A growing Christian who lives his life according to God's Word will be quick to listen, slow to speak, and slow to get angry. Why does James emphasize these qualities? He does so because in times of testing and temptation, our natural human tendency is to reverse these qualities. We naturally tend to be slow to listen, quick to speak, and quick to become angry.

Quick to listen

We are not inclined to listen—but boy, do we want to be heard! When angered or frustrated, our tendency is to fuss and fume, to unleash our anger, to lash out and punish someone. Satan understands our natural human tendencies better than we do. He uses our times of testing to worm his way into our thinking, applying pressure and prompting us to act impulsively, without listening, without thinking, without submitting to God's Word. Because we tend to act and speak without listening, we easily fall into temptation. That's why Jesus taught us to pray, "And lead us not into temptation, but deliver us from evil."

When Satan tempted Jesus, what did he do? He came to Jesus at the point of his most urgent and immediate need. Led by the Spirit, Jesus went into the wilderness and ate nothing for forty days. So Satan said to him, "If you are the Son of God, command this stone to become bread" (Luke 4:3). Satan was saying to Jesus, "You can do it, so do it now. You don't have to live in dependence on God; you can act independently of the Father."

Whether you are aware of it or not, you face similar temptations from time to time. You face tough times in your life, and your anxiety level rises. You wonder, *What if God doesn't come through for me? What if he doesn't provide?* As your suffering increases and your anxiety grows, you are strongly tempted to listen to other voices and ignore the voice of God. Sometimes you are even tempted through well-meaning but misguided advice from other Christians.

It's wise to seek the advice of other believers when we are contemplating a difficult decision—but the advice of fellow believers is not infallible. In Acts 21, Paul feels compelled to go to Jerusalem, yet the Christians he meets along the way keep telling him he should *not* go there because he will be arrested and imprisoned. These believers offer good, sound, sensible advice, and if comfort and safety were all that mattered to Paul, he would have taken their advice. But Paul knew that God had called him to Jerusalem for a reason, and that even his arrest and imprisonment would have a purpose.

Though the believers Paul met were correct in understanding that Paul would suffer if he went to Jerusalem, they were mistaken in thinking that Paul should not go. They loved Paul and wanted to spare him from suffering, imprisonment, and death. But Paul knew that God could use his suffering to advance the gospel. And, in fact, some of Paul's most powerful, instructive, and comforting epistles— Ephesians, Philippians, Colossians, and Philemon—were written when he was in prison.

Fellow Christians will often give you advice that is reasonable, logical, and motivated by their genuine love for you. The advice Satan gave Jesus when he was hungry in the wilderness also seemed reasonable and logical: "If you are the Son of God, command this stone to become bread." If Jesus could do so, why shouldn't he? But Jesus analyzed Satan's advice in light of God's Word and replied, "It is written, 'Man shall not live by bread alone'" (Luke 4:4).

How can you know if the voice you hear is the voice of the Lord or the temptation of Satan? The test is simple: If it is the voice of the Lord, everything that voice says will be compatible and consistent with the Word of God. The Holy Spirit will never tell you to do anything that is inconsistent with the Scriptures.

Slow to speak, slow to get angry

When we go through a time of testing, our natural reaction is to say things we shouldn't say. We complain about God. We accuse him of unfairness, of lacking compassion, of abandoning us. When we complain about God, that is the sin of rebellion. As you read the books of Exodus through Deuteronomy, you see again and again that God must discipline his people because of their murmuring and complaining against him.

This doesn't mean there is no place for crying out to God in our grief, despair, or anger. As you read through the Psalms, for example, you will find many "lament psalms" (for examples, Psalm 3, 12, 22, 44, 57, 74, 80, and 139). In these passages of Scripture, the psalmist cries out to God about the ferocity of his foes, the destructive lies spread by his enemies, his feelings of loneliness and the pain of feeling forsaken, and on and on. Though it is a sin to complain *about* God, it is an act of prayerful faith and worship to bring our laments and problems *before* God.

Immature Christians expect a life of ease, and they whine and gripe and accuse God whenever things don't go their way. Mature, growing Christians understand the place of suffering in this life, and they know that God welcomes and understands their prayers for deliverance, strength, healing, comfort, and salvation. Mature Christians also know they should be slow to speak. As the ancient proverb reminds us, God created us with two ears and one mouth so that we would listen twice as much as we talk.

James also tells us that we should be slow to anger. There are very few Christians who have truly mastered the art of being slow to anger—myself included! There have been times in my life when it could be truthfully said that "my mouth runneth over" and "my ears stoppeth up." It took me many years to realize what a fool I was to be quick to anger—and it is still easy to fall into old patterns of behavior if I have not gone to the Lord in prayer, asking for a fresh filling of the Holy Spirit.

Why does James tell us there is no place for hasty, thoughtless speech and rage and anger in the life of the believer? Why does James give us this threefold command to be quick to hear, slow to speak, slow to anger? In verse 20, James explains, "for the anger of man does not produce the righteousness of God." The righteousness of God cannot be accomplished in us through human anger. We cannot become what God wants us to be as long as we are spitting and sputtering with rage.

The Scriptures contain many examples of men and women who allowed their anger to blemish their relationship with God. Cain became angry when God would not accept his offering—and his anger compelled him to strike out against his obedient brother, Abel, and murder him in a fit of rage (see Genesis 4). Moses became angry with the people of Israel when they quarreled with him and murmured against God, so instead of commanding the rock to bring forth water, he struck the rock with his staff—and God told Moses he would not be allowed to lead the people into the land of promise (see Numbers 20). The prophet Jonah became angry after the people of Nineveh repented and God chose not to destroy them. Instead of celebrating the love and grace of God, Jonah sat under a large shady plant and sulked (see Jonah 4).

Human anger blinds us to the will of God, the grace of God, and the love of God. Human anger renders us unresponsive to God's leading, often with terrible consequences. Anger makes us feel justified in doing unjustifiable acts. A Christian who would never think of committing an act of violence might spread rumors and destroy reputations and feel righteous and justified in doing so because of anger. Until you surrender your anger to God, he cannot use you and bless you.

Doers of the Word

How should we respond when tests or temptations threaten our walk with Christ? In verse 21, James counsels us to take twofold action: "Therefore put away all filthiness and rampant wickedness and receive with meekness the implanted word, which is able to save your souls." The two actions James tells us to take are (1) put away all evil and (2) receive the implanted Word of God.

Imagine the human heart is a garden that needs care and cultivation. If left to itself, the soil of this garden will produce only weeds. James tells us, first, to pull out the weeds by putting away "all filthiness and rampant wickedness." In this way we prepare the soil of the garden to receive the implanted Word of God.

Just as it would be foolish to plant good seed in a patch of ground that is overrun with weeds, it would be utter foolishness to try to receive God's Word into our lives as long as our hearts are overgrown with anger, bitterness, envy, and resentment. These weeds choke off the seed of the Word. The Word of God cannot have its effect on our lives if we have not pulled out the weeds of sin.

How do we rid ourselves of these weeds? We begin by confessing our sin and asking God to forgive us. Second, we ask God to come into our lives and soften our hearts to receive his Word. This is like a farmer plowing the field, breaking up the soil so that the seed can be planted. Third, we ask God in prayer to allow his Word to impact our lives and take hold in such a way that the weeds cannot grow back and choke out our spiritual life.

How does the Word of God impact our lives? How does God's Word prevent the weeds of sin from growing back? It certainly doesn't happen if we merely open the Bible for a quick ten-minute glance every now and then. Francis Cosgrove, in his book *The Essentials of Discipleship*, offered these questions designed to enable our study of God's Word to have a deeper impact on our lives:

Ask yourself these questions about the passage you are reading:

- Is there an example for me to follow?
- Is there a command for me to obey?
- Is there any error for me to avoid?
- Is there any sin for me to renounce?
- Is there any promise for me to claim?
- Is there any new thought about God himself?
- Is there any new thought about Jesus Christ?
- Is there any new thought about the Holy Spirit's ministry in my life?[6]

Notice that James writes that we must "receive *with meekness* the implanted word." What does "with meekness" mean? Many people equate meekness with weakness. But that is not what God's Word means by that term. Meekness means we are to receive God's Word with a sense of acceptance. It means we don't argue with God's Word or twist God's Word to make it conform to our thinking. Instead, we honor God's Word as truth. We receive it, accept it, and obey it. As James goes on to write:

> But be doers of the word, and not hearers only, deceiving yourselves. For if anyone is a hearer of the word and not a doer, he is like a man who looks intently at his natural face in a mirror. For he looks at himself and goes away and at once forgets what he was like. But the one who looks into the perfect law, the law of liberty, and perseveres, being no hearer who forgets but a doer who acts, he will be blessed in his doing (1:22-25).

James is talking about those who read the Bible regularly but whose lives are no different from the lives of unbelievers. They hear sermons, go to midweek Bible studies, and keep a Bible on their nightstand—but the Word of God has no impact or influence on the way they live. They fill their minds with the same filth their worldly counterparts wallow in. They tell the same jokes, use the same filthy speech, they cheat the boss and the government, and maybe even cheat on their spouses. What is the point of reading God's Word when it has no effect on their daily lives?

James compares this sort of person with someone who looks in a mirror—then instantly forgets what he sees. So he goes around with uncombed hair, an unshaven chin, and spinach in his teeth. Looking in the mirror didn't do him any good at all because he didn't use his time at the mirror to improve his personal hygiene and appearance.

Such a person goes through his day and can't understand why people point and stare and ask, "What happened to you?" He says, "There's nothing wrong with me. I looked in the mirror this morning.

I'm fine." But he's not fine because he didn't act on what the mirror showed him. A mirror has a purpose, which is to show you what you need to do in order to make yourself presentable to the world. And the purpose of the Word of God is to show you what you need to do to make yourself spiritually presentable to others and to God. All the time you spend reading the Bible won't do you any good if you are not willing to obey what you read.

Like a mirror, God's Word confronts us with our flaws, not so that we will feel bad about ourselves, but so that we can correct those flaws. When we look at the Bible, we see our faults, our sins, our jealousies, our greed, our idolatries, the wrongs we commit toward others, and the weakness of our faith. The Bible exposes our sins so that we can ask God to cleanse us and remove our flaws and blemishes.

In Exodus 30, we read of a bronze basin that stood between the tent of meeting and the altar. It was filled with water, and priests would cleanse themselves in that basin before entering the holy place to minister before the Lord. Water for washing is a picture of the cleansing Word of God—the Word that we not only hear but obey. As Jesus said in John 15:3, "Already you are clean because of the word that I have spoken to you." And Paul said that the Lord Jesus "loved the church and gave himself up for her, that he might sanctify her, having cleansed her by the washing of water with the word" (Ephesians 5:25-26).

People who hear the Word but do not obey it are candidates for frustration. As someone said, impression without expression leads to depression. So let us not be hearers of the Word only, but also doers of the Word.

Religion that is pure and undefiled

Six hundred years before Christ, the prophet Ezekiel preached to the children of Israel. The audience sat before him, soaking up his words. But God saw the hearts of the people—and he didn't like what he saw. So God spoke to Ezekiel, saying, "And they come to you as people come, and they sit before you as my people, and they hear what you say but they will not do it; for with lustful talk in their mouths they act; their heart is set on their gain" (Ezekiel 33:31).

How does obedience to the Word of God manifest itself? What is the fruit of not only hearing the Word but also doing it? What is the outward manifestation of our claim to follow Christ? James goes on to tell us:

> If anyone thinks he is religious and does not bridle his tongue but deceives his heart, this person's religion is worthless. Religion that is pure and undefiled before God, the Father, is this: to visit orphans and widows in their affliction, and to keep oneself unstained from the world (1:26-27).

When James talks about "religion" here, the word has nothing to do with ceremonies and rituals. "Religion that is pure and undefiled" means the practice of God's Word, the act of living it out and sharing it with others. How do you do that? James gives us three characteristics that reveal what pure, undefiled religion looks like.

The *first characteristic* of a "religion that is pure and undefiled" is the ability to bridle or control the tongue. James says that anyone who claims to be religious but does not keep his or her tongue under control is living a worthless and meaningless religion (James will delve into this subject in greater detail in chapter 3 of this epistle). Why is our speech so important to God? Because *the tongue reveals what is in the heart.*

The words of your mouth reveal the state of your heart. If your lips are not moving in praise to God, then your heart is not really thankful. If your lips are always criticizing, then a critical spirit is behind those lips. If your mouth is spewing curses, it's because your heart has not come under the control of God.

Do you criticize or encourage? Do you bless or curse? Do you build up or tear down? Jesus said, "For out of the abundance of the heart the mouth speaks" (Matthew 12:34).

The *second characteristic* of a "religion that is pure and undefiled" is genuine compassion expressed in authentic caring action. "Religion that is pure and undefiled before God, the Father," James writes, "is this: to visit orphans and widows in their affliction." Compassion is love in action—not just words but deeds of the heart, hands, resources, and talent. It means doing acts of love toward others; it means you don't merely get wrapped up in yourself and your plans; it means you don't merely say "I'll pray for you" as an excuse for doing nothing.

When you hear a sermon or read a passage of Scripture that convicts your soul in a powerful way, and you sense that God is giving you a bold new insight or command—what should you do? Should you keep it to yourself? No! You want to share those new insights with others. God blesses us through his Word in order that we may be a blessing to others.

This is equally true in the realm of material blessings. God blesses you financially and materially so that you might be a blessing to others. That is a biblical principle. God doesn't give us blessings for purely selfish use; he wants us to use our blessings to bless others. He wants us to "visit orphans and widows in their affliction." He wants us to share our blessings with people in need.

The *third characteristic* of a "religion that is pure and undefiled" is separation from the world. James writes that authentic religion is "to keep oneself unstained from the world." Authentic Christians are *in* the world but remain unspotted and undefiled *by* the world. The Greek word translated "world" here refers to the secular culture, the society that is without God. It's the same word Paul uses in Ephesians 2:2 when he speaks of those who follow "the course of this world, following the prince of the power of the air, the spirit that is now at work in the sons of disobedience."

How do we separate ourselves from the world? Do we run off and join a mountaintop monastery? Do we surround ourselves with a plastic bubble? No. The very fact that James tells us to remain unstained by the world suggests that we must be in the world yet constantly on our guard against spiritual contamination. We are like spiritual astronauts—willing to venture into an environment that is spiritually hostile and deadly because we have sealed ourselves up in a "spacesuit" of pure and undefiled religion, and we constantly breathe the life-giving atmosphere of God's Word.

Keeping ourselves unstained by the world means that, as genuine Christians, we will stand out. We will be conspicuous. We will attract attention. And yes, we will attract ridicule and mockery. Even though we may suffer rejection and persecution, we will continue to stand tall for God and for his gospel.

This means we will often be tempted to compromise, to soft-pedal our faith, to mute our witness, to try to blend in a little more with the world. If you compromise on one issue of your faith, then the temptation will grow to compromise others. The pressure to compromise may come from the people around you or it may come from within, from your own anxious desire to be accepted and approved by others. And you will begin to compromise in this area and that area—and before you know it, you are conforming to the world's standards. Your witness for Christ has been silenced.

We see this principle in the life of Lot, Abraham's nephew, whose story is told in Genesis 11 through 14 and 19. Lot initially made camp on the fertile Jordan plain. A number of cities were on the plain, and Lot pitched his tent toward Sodom so that he could do business with that city. Over time, he moved his tent closer and closer to Sodom, until his tent overlooked Sodom, and finally—Lot moved right into town!

Instead of standing apart from Sodom and its sins, Lot became one of the leading citizens of Sodom. Genesis 19:1 describes Lot as "sitting in the gate of Sodom," a phrase many Bible scholars interpret as meaning that Lot had become a municipal judge or city official in Sodom. Later, one of the citizens of Sodom complains that Lot "came to sojourn, and he has become the judge!" (19:9). In any case, it is clear that Lot gradually compromised with Sodom until he lost his distinctiveness and his testimony for God, until even his own family lost respect for him. When God's judgment fell upon Sodom, Lot lost everything he owned.

Contrast the story of Lot with the story of our Lord Jesus. The Lord was in the world, but not of it. He remained sinless, unblemished, and undefiled by the world, yet it was said of him that he was a friend of sinners. He never compromised his moral stance—yet sinners loved to be with him.

That is the kind of uncompromising, pure, undefiled, yet attractive religion that you and I must live out as witnesses in this dying world. To our neighbors, you and I are walking, talking Bibles, perhaps the only Bible they will ever hear or read. So let's make sure that the lives we lead are consistent with the message we read in God's Word. Let's live as Jesus lived—in the world but not of it, uncompromising but attractive, undefiled by sin but friends to sinners, keeping ourselves unstained by the world.

4

Loving the Unlovable

During the Korean War, communist North Korean forces overran a South Korean village. As part of the communist campaign of terror, the young North Korean officer in charge ordered the arrest of community leaders. One of those arrested was a Korean Christian man who operated an orphanage.

When the communist officer learned that the Christian man cared for orphans, he decided to spare the man's life. But he still wanted to cultivate fear, so he forced the orphanage director to watch as they executed his nineteen-year-old son in cold blood.

Eventually, the Korean War wound down to a stalemate. The young communist officer was captured and tried for war crimes before a United Nations tribunal. He was convicted—but before the sentence could be imposed, the orphanage director went before the tribunal and pleaded for the life of the man who had executed his son. "This young officer didn't really know what he was doing," he said. "Give him to me, and I will train him."

The tribunal released the prisoner into the custody of the

orphanage director. True to his word, the Christian man taught and discipled this former enemy who had killed his son. The former communist went on to become a prominent pastor in the South Korean church.[7]

Could you have forgiven the man who took your son's life? Could you have pleaded for his life before a military tribunal? Could you have received him into your home? Could you have accepted the challenge of loving, forgiving, and discipling such an enemy?

Yet this, in fact, is what God has done for you and me. Our sins nailed his Son to the cross. Our sins murdered the Son of God. And God loves us, forgives us, disciples us, and sends us out to spread the story of his love and forgiveness to the world.

He has sent us out on a mission to love the unlovable, forgive the unforgivable, and draw sinners into his kingdom.

Power brokers and bosses

As we plunge into the second chapter of James, the apostle tells us that we are not only to love those who love us back. We are not only to love those who are easy to love. We are not only to love those who can benefit us. We are to love the unlovable.

Loving the unlovable does not come naturally. It is a learned response. Our natural response is to love the beautiful people, the loving people, the influential people. We tend to love those who are in a position to help us or advance our agenda in some way. That is why, even in the church, we exhibit an all-too-human tendency to show partiality to the lovable people while ignoring and even snubbing the unlovable. So James writes:

> My brothers, show no partiality as you hold the faith in our Lord Jesus Christ, the Lord of glory. For if a man wearing a gold ring and fine clothing comes into your assembly, and a poor man in shabby clothing also comes in, and if you pay attention to the one who wears the fine clothing and say, "You sit here in a good place,"

while you say to the poor man, "You stand over there," or, "Sit down at my feet," have you not then made distinctions among yourselves and become judges with evil thoughts? Listen, my beloved brothers, has not God chosen those who are poor in the world to be rich in faith and heirs of the kingdom, which he has promised to those who love him? But you have dishonored the poor man. Are not the rich the ones who oppress you, and the ones who drag you into court? Are they not the ones who blaspheme the honorable name by which you were called? (2:1-7).

In the first century, just as in the twenty-first century, people craved recognition and honor. They vied with one another for praise. Jesus denounced such attitudes when he said that the scribes and Pharisees "love the place of honor at feasts and the best seats in the synagogues and greetings in the marketplaces and being called rabbi by others…Whoever exalts himself will be humbled, and whoever humbles himself will be exalted" (Matthew 23:6-7,12).

We have these same sorts of pyramid climbers in the church today. Now as then, many want to have prominence and control in the church. They want to become spiritual teachers and leaders, and they want these positions for the wrong reasons—to win praise and respect and status, to enlarge their own egos and reputations. And if they don't receive the prominence and power they crave in one church, they move on and seek it in another.

James tells us that the church does not exist to feed people's egos, and we must not let those who seek power and prominence get away with it. Attention-seeking pride is a spiritual disease that can spread harm to the entire congregation. In the church of Jesus Christ, only Jesus deserves the prominence. In the church, only Jesus has the right to be in control. In the church, our focus should be on Jesus, not on any human leader.

Jesus was no respecter of persons. Even his enemies said to him, "you do not care about anyone's opinion, for you are not swayed by appearances" (Matthew 22:16). Our Lord did not permit the power-hungry attention-seekers to get away with it.

Many churches, both in the first and the twenty-first centuries, have failed to learn this lesson. There are people in churches who are accustomed to getting their way. When they speak, even the pastor and the church board listen. These individuals often become the unofficial power brokers, the "church bosses" who hide behind the scenes and push the buttons and pull the levers of the church machinery.

Because Jesus was no respecter of persons, we must not show partiality in the church. The church must reflect the personality of Jesus himself. So we must not allow ourselves to be intimidated, awed, or swept off our feet by those who seek power. James uses symbolic imagery to depict such people, picturing them as wearing gold rings and fine clothing. In the church today, it may not be as easy to identify such people by their jewelry and clothing, but they do give themselves away.

The power brokers and attention seekers will, sooner or later, try to impose their will upon the church. They will let it be known that their ideas are better, their methods smarter, their plans more reliable, their solutions more dependable. Some will use their wealth—their tithes and donations—to control what takes place in the church.

If we truly hold to the teachings of the Lord Jesus Christ, if we are living out Christlike character and values, then our priorities should be his priorities, our message should be his message, our actions should be like his. If Jesus showed no partiality, then how dare we treat some people in the church as more important than others? How dare we let rich, powerful "bosses" in the church intimidate us into compromising our Christlike character? As James himself says, "But you have dishonored the poor man. Are not the rich the ones who oppress you, and the ones who drag you into court?

Are they not the ones who blaspheme the honorable name by which you were called?"

Nobody owns a church

In the classic Walt Disney motion picture *Pollyanna*, we meet a young orphan, Pollyanna (Hayley Mills), whose missionary parents have died. Pollyanna goes to live with her wealthy Aunt Polly (Jane Wyman). Everyone in the town kowtows to Aunt Polly because of her wealth and influence. Even Reverend Ford (Karl Malden) obeys her every whim and preaches the sermons Polly tells him to preach. He doesn't dare oppose her on any matter because she holds all the power in the church.

Reverend Ford soon finds himself in a dilemma between what is best for the church and what the iron-willed Aunt Polly demands of him. He makes fine-sounding excuses for always giving in to her wishes—until one day, Pollyanna tells Reverend Ford, in her innocent way, "Nobody owns a church."

When Reverend Ford hears those words, his conscience is laid bare. He realizes that he has been a coward all these years, and he has treated Aunt Polly as if she owns the church. Pollyanna's simple statement is the turning point for Reverend Ford. From that moment on, he no longer serves the will of Aunt Polly. He begins to serve the Lord.

It's a simple yet profound insight: no human being owns the church. The church is the bride and the possession of Jesus Christ alone. That is the theme of James 2.

Throughout the years that I have been pastor of The Church of The Apostles, I have felt pressure at times to use worldly marketing techniques and public opinion surveys in an attempt to make our church's ministry more "relevant" to this or that segment of the population. I have been urged to kowtow to certain groups or individuals. The temptation is strong. But I am always reminded of the words of Jesus and James—and the words of Proverbs 22:2: "The rich and the poor meet together; the LORD is the maker of them all."

When Jesus founded his church, he never intended that it would be run according to the standards and principles of the world. We have an obligation not to bring worldly standards into his church. We must not set out to please powerful individuals or cliques. As Christians, we are to please one person, the Lord Jesus Christ.

To show partiality, to treat some in the church as more favored and entitled than others, is to make distinctions among ourselves and to become "judges with evil thoughts." It means that we have two sets of rules in the church—one set of rules for the rich and powerful and another for the poor. To have two sets of rules is to be "double-minded," and James has already told us in James 1:8 that to be double-minded is to be unstable in all our ways.

When we show partiality, we indicate that we are living by our old minds rather than by the new nature we have received from Christ. Showing partiality indicates that we are not thinking with the mind of Jesus.

Loving others as God loves us

One of the challenges of parenting is to treat your children impartially, without any appearance of unfairness or favoritism. You will never convince your kids that you are being impartial. The youngest will accuse you of favoring the oldest because he has more privileges. The oldest will accuse you of babying the youngest. They will fight for attention, praise, privileges, and more allowance—and complain that they have too many chores. Even so, our goal as Christian parents should be to represent God, our loving heavenly Father, to our children—to treat them impartially and to love them as unconditionally as God loves us.

I was deeply moved by the story of a godly Christian man who was told by doctors that his beloved young son was terminally ill. Shocked and saddened, the father wondered how to break the news to his little boy. The one great comfort this father had was that his boy had accepted Christ as his Savior. He knew his son's death would be a transition to glory in the presence of the Lord.

But he couldn't imagine how he would tell his son that his earthly life would be cut short. So he prayed and asked the Holy Spirit for guidance. Then he went to his son's bedside. He began by reading a passage from Scripture and praying with his son. Then he gently explained the medical diagnosis to the boy. His son took the news sadly but bravely.

"Son," the father asked, "are you afraid to meet Jesus?"

"No, Dad," the boy replied, "not if he's like you."

In the midst of almost incomprehensible grief, this father experienced the joy of knowing that his son had seen Christ in him.

That's what James is saying to us in this passage. Our lives should reflect Jesus Christ. Our churches should reflect Jesus Christ. When the world looks at Christians and the Christian church, it should not see just another worldly organization, operating by the same rules as the secular world. The world should see people who love others unconditionally, who accept others without favoritism, who are not intimidated by wealth, power, and position.

Why is it so important that we love one another unconditionally and that we refuse to show partiality and favoritism in the church? James explains, "Listen, my beloved brothers, has not God chosen those who are poor in the world to be rich in faith and heirs of the kingdom, which he has promised to those who love him? But you have dishonored the poor man" (2:5-6a). When we show favoritism to the rich, we dishonor the poor and powerless.

In order to truly be like Christ, we must love all people the same. We must honor the people Jesus most identified with—the poor, the gentle, and the meek.

The "royal law" of love

The apostle James goes on to write of what he calls the "royal law" of Scripture:

> If you really fulfill the royal law according to the Scripture, "You shall love your neighbor as yourself," you are doing well. But if you show partiality, you are committing sin and are convicted by the law as transgressors. For whoever keeps the whole law but fails in one point has become accountable for all of it. For he who said, "Do not commit adultery," also said, "Do not murder." If you do not commit adultery but do murder, you have become a transgressor of the law. So speak and so act as those who are to be judged under the law of liberty. For judgment is without mercy to one who has shown no mercy. Mercy triumphs over judgment (2:8-13).

If we are truly carrying out the demands of the royal law of Scripture—"You shall love your neighbor as yourself"—then we will ask ourselves, *Who do I want to please? Do I want to please the rich and powerful? Or do I want to please the Lord Jesus Christ?* If I truly want to please the Lord, I will show no favoritism. I will love everyone equally, just as he loved everyone equally.

You might ask, "Did Jesus truly love everyone equally?" After all, Jesus spent more time with the Twelve than with the hundred and twenty disciples. He spent more time with three (Peter, James, and John) than he spent with the Twelve. And he spent more time with John than with the three. Nevertheless, he loved all people equally and without favoritism. The time he allocated to different people was a matter of investing in lives, not favoring one person over another. The ground is level at the foot of the cross.

Why does James call this commandment, "You shall love your neighbor as yourself," the "royal law"? It's because this law was given by the King. God the Father gave us this law in Leviticus 19:18. God the Son reaffirmed this law to his disciples (see Matthew 22:39, Mark

12:31, Luke 10:27, and John 13:34-35). And God the Spirit enables us to practice the "royal law" with all people, including unlovable people, "because God's love has been poured into our hearts through the Holy Spirit who has been given to us" (Romans 5:5b).

Another reason this is called the "royal law" is because it rules over all other laws. If you follow this law and love your neighbor as you love yourself, you hardly need any other law. If you practice the "royal law," you will never run afoul of the laws that tell you not to steal, not to kill, and not to commit adultery.

But there is yet another reason why this law is called the "royal law"—and that is because it truly makes you a king. Think about it: Hatred makes you a slave—a slave of the person you hate. Who dominates your thinking? The person you hate! Who consumes your mental and emotional energy? The person you hate!

Hate makes you a slave. Love sets you free. Love enables you to reign like a king.

In much the same way, showing partiality makes you a slave. When you are a respecter of persons, you are constantly trying to please and impress others. You are afraid of offending or upsetting others. You cannot speak candidly. You cannot be yourself. Only when you begin treating all people impartially do you truly experience absolute freedom.

You might say, "I wish I could love people unconditionally. I wish I could love unlovable people. But you don't know the kind of people I have to deal with. You don't know how harsh and unreasonable my spouse is. You don't know what a tyrant my boss is. You don't know how ungrateful and spiteful my child is. You don't know how rude and mean my professor is."

You're right. I don't know the various unlovely and unlovable people in your life. But I do know this: God's Word tells us that he has given us the power to live out the "royal law" with all the people in our lives "because God's love has been poured into our hearts through the Holy Spirit who has been given to us." You may not be able to love that unlovable person in your life, but if you call upon God's Holy Spirit, he will love that unlovable person through you. Think of the Spirit as the hand of God, and you are the glove. Let the Spirit come into your life and fill you like the hand filling the glove. Let the Spirit touch that person's life and grip that person with the love of God. Let the Spirit fill your heart, spirit, mind, and emotions as a hand fills a glove, and let the Spirit do the work that is impossible for a human being to do. Let the Spirit conform your love to his love.

To love someone with a Christlike love does not mean you have to like that person. It doesn't mean you have to agree with that person. It doesn't mean you have to accept that person's vile words, hurtful actions, or destructive habits. To love that person with the love of Christ does not necessarily mean that you are going to be an intimate friend of that person.

But it does mean that you will treat that person in a loving way, just as God has treated you and me. And how did God treat us? The Scriptures tell us, "but God shows his love for us in that while we were still sinners, Christ died for us" (Romans 5:8).

God did not say to us, "You change—and then I will love you." He loved us first, while we were still in rebellion against him. He loved us even though we hated him. He loved us even though we sinned against him. He loved us even while we were nailing his Son to the cross.

That is how we are to love the unlovable people in our lives. That kind of love is not an emotional experience. We can't manufacture warm fuzzy feelings for people who repeatedly hurt us, hate us, and curse us. Loving others with the love of Christ has nothing to do with pasting a fake smile on our faces.

The love of Christ is not a feeling. The love of Christ is an act of the will. We love unlovable people in order to glorify God. We love them out of gratitude for the unconditional love of God for us. We love them through the power of the Holy Spirit.

This love is what the writers of the Greek New Testament call *agape*. This kind of love is so foreign and unnatural to human experience that there was no word to describe it in the first-century world. The writers of the New Testament had to take an obscure word that had rarely appeared in Greek literature and use it to describe this new kind of love—Christlike love, unconditional love, love that is an act of the will, not a feeling or emotion.

To love the unlovely is simply unnatural. That is why this kind of love can come only from a supernatural source, from the Holy Spirit himself. That's why this love is listed first among the fruit of the Spirit in Galatians 5:22-23. And the amazing thing about this supernatural love is that, as we act in *agape*-love toward one another, we may actually find that feelings of affection will follow. We may find ourselves feeling drawn to people we once saw as unlovable. We may learn to see such people in a totally new light.

The law of liberty

How do we know that *agape*-love is an act of the will, not an emotional feeling? Because James tells us that our deeds, our actions, will be judged: "So speak and so act as those who are to be judged under the law of liberty. For judgment is without mercy to one who has shown no mercy. Mercy triumphs over judgment."

We cannot always control our feelings and emotions. If someone strikes us, spits on us, curses us, ignores us, or rejects us, we will feel hurt. Those hurt feelings may be accompanied by sorrow or anger—and we can't always control our feelings. *But we can control our actions.*

God will not judge us for feeling hurt because someone abused us. But if we lash out, if we seek revenge, if we curse, if we hold a grudge, our deeds will be judged. While it is true that there is no condemnation for those who are in Christ Jesus (see Romans 8:1), our sins affect our character. We can't expect to serve God faithfully and productively while we sin against his royal law of love. God forgives our sins as we confess them, but forgiveness does not alter the natural consequences of sin.

And even though we cannot always control our feelings, God does expect us to control our attitude. As James tells us in verse 13, God judges our attitude as well as our deeds—and God expects us to maintain an attitude of mercy even toward people who hate us and hurt us. "For judgment is without mercy to one who has shown no mercy," James writes. "Mercy triumphs over judgment."

It's important that we understand what James is telling us when he writes, "So speak and so act as those who are to be judged under the law of liberty" (2:12). It's vitally important that we understand God's law of liberty—what it is and what it is not. The law of liberty is not a license to sin, liberally and freely. Rather, it is the freedom God has given us that liberates us from slavery to sin.

Because God has loved us with an unconditional love, we are no longer slaves to sin. Through the power of the Holy Spirit, God's Word can change our hearts and enable us to love the unlovable. As the fruit of the Spirit becomes increasingly evident in our lives, we will find that we are able to love unlovable people not out of a sense of duty or obligation, but out of a genuine desire to please God and do his will.

One of the tests of the reality of our faith is our ability to love the people in our lives who are unlovely and unlovable. Can we pass the test?

5

Faith that Works

The Protestant Reformation began when one man, Martin Luther (1483–1546), rediscovered the doctrine of faith. The church in medieval times had wandered so far from God's Word that it actually taught that people could escape God's punishment for sin through good works, including the performance of rites and rituals of the church. The church even taught that full or partial remission of sin could be purchased for cash through so-called "indulgences"—a kind of spiritual Ponzi scheme the church hierarchy used to finance the construction of elaborate cathedrals.

Martin Luther, a German monk and a brilliant Bible scholar, was reading in Romans 1 when he was struck by these words of the apostle Paul: "For I am not ashamed of the gospel, for it is the power of God for salvation to everyone who believes, to the Jew first and also to the Greek. For in it the righteousness of God is revealed from faith for faith, as it is written, 'The righteous shall live by faith'" (Romans 1:16-17).

Luther had read those words many times before, but this time,

the meaning of those words jumped out at him in a fresh and powerful way: "The righteous shall live by faith"! In Romans, and also in
Galatians 3:11, Paul echoed the Old Testament prophecy of Habak-
kuk 2:4: "but the righteous shall live by his faith." Luther also realized that this emphasis on faith dovetailed with the words of Jesus
to Nicodemus: "For God so loved the world, that he gave his only
Son, *that whoever believes in him should not perish but have eternal
life*" (John 3:16, emphasis added).

It must have come as an incredible shock for Martin Luther to
realize that the teachings he had lived by and taught to others were
at odds with the teachings of God's own Word. Suddenly he understood why, even as a scholar in the church, he had never had any
assurance that his sins were forgiven. Suddenly he understood that
the sale of indulgences, which permitted the rich to buy absolution
while condemning the poor to purgatory or hell, made absolutely
no sense according to Scripture. The moment he realized that the
righteous shall live by faith, the light of the gospel broke through
the clouds of his confusion and illuminated his soul.

The rediscovery of *faith* as the mechanism of salvation was the
spark that ignited the Protestant Reformation. Six centuries have
come and gone since Martin Luther made his world-changing rediscovery of faith. Yet even today, many still teach the erroneous doctrine that salvation is a matter of human works. In James 2, the
apostle demolishes that false doctrine and explains the delicate balance between faith and works.

Actions speak louder than words

Here we come to one of the most famous passages in the epistle of James. It's a passage that has often been misinterpreted over
the years, even though its meaning is not difficult or obscure in any
way. James writes:

> What good is it, my brothers, if someone says he has
> faith but does not have works? Can that faith save him?

If a brother or sister is poorly clothed and lacking in daily food, and one of you says to them, "Go in peace, be warmed and filled," without giving them the things needed for the body, what good is that? So also faith by itself, if it does not have works, is dead.

But someone will say, "You have faith and I have works." Show me your faith apart from your works, and I will show you my faith by my works. You believe that God is one; you do well. Even the demons believe—and shudder! (2:14-19).

In a world dominated by the idea that salvation must be earned by good works, James places spiritual reality in its proper perspective. While he stipulates that salvation is by faith, he makes it clear what faith is—and what it is not. Is faith simply a matter of agreeing with a doctrine or creed? Is faith merely a matter of giving mental assent to a list of orthodox theological positions? James emphatically says "No!"

If a person has genuinely experienced saving faith, that person will manifest the fruit of faith. In other words, the works that person does will be consistent with the faith he or she professes. Faith saves us, but works prove our faith is genuine. If we say, "I believe in Jesus Christ," yet we do the works of Satan, which is the more reliable indicator of our spiritual condition—our words or our works?

Some critics of the Bible seize on this passage and claim that James contradicts Paul, who writes, "yet we know that a person is not justified by works of the law but through faith in Jesus Christ, so we also have believed in Christ Jesus, in order to be justified by faith in Christ and not by works of the law, because by works of the law no one will be justified" (Galatians 2:16). The skeptics compare the words of Paul against the words of James and say, "You see? Paul teaches salvation by faith alone, but James teaches salvation by works."

The only way you can claim that James and Paul contradict each other is by interpreting both writers either carelessly or dishonestly. The key words in James 2 are: "if someone says he has faith." James is saying, in other words, "Watch out for those who claim to be believers, yet whose lifestyle does not match up with the Christian faith." Another way to paraphrase James is the old adage, "Actions speak louder than words."

The Christian gospel is often presented as a matter of simple believism: If you believe certain doctrines about Jesus, then you are saved. Sometimes, Christian preachers and evangelists present the gospel in a way that suggests that all you have to do is "receive Jesus as your Savior," and you are saved. I'm convinced it's a tragic mistake to preach Jesus as Savior without preaching him as Lord. We all need to ask ourselves, "If Jesus is not the Lord of my life, then is he truly my Savior?"

I'm not saying that if Jesus is your Lord you will never sin or stumble. I'm saying that if Jesus is truly the Lord of your life, you will always repent and return to him. Authentic faith will make a difference in your life—a difference that people will be able to see.

Many people make the mistake of thinking that James is writing here about works. If you step back from this passage and look at the broad scope of James's message, you see that he is actually writing about faith. He is showing us what genuine faith looks like. He is making sure that we don't mistake "easy believism" (so-called faith that is not backed up by action) for the genuine article. He wants us to know that any so-called faith that does not affect the way we live is dead and is not worthy to be called faith.

The epistle of James may talk about works, but it is all about faith.

The testimony of a "Christian gangster"

Mickey Cohen was a notorious gangster in Hollywood in the 1940s and 1950s. One of Cohen's partners in crime was Jim Vaus, a wiretapper for the mob. In the early 1950s, Vaus attended a Billy Graham Crusade, and under the conviction of the Holy Spirit he went forward and gave his life to Christ. Vaus gave up his life of crime, and even sold his home, his car, and other possessions in order to make restitution for his crimes. He eventually founded a discipleship organization, Youth Development, Inc., that continues to train Christian young people today.

Jim Vaus told Cohen about his conversion to Christ. Cohen was interested in the gospel and attended a private meeting with Billy Graham and a number of Hollywood notables, including western stars Stuart Hamblen, Roy Rogers, and Dale Evans. Mickey Cohen responded to Dr. Graham's invitation to accept Christ—and for a few days, it seemed that the gangster had made a serious decision to follow Christ.

But soon after making that decision, Cohen was again hanging out with his friends in the mob and still engaging in underworld activities. When Jim Vaus and members of the Graham evangelistic team explained to Cohen that he could not be a Christian and go on living as a mobster, he replied, "You never told me that I had to give up my career. You never told me that I had to give up my friends. There are Christian movie stars, Christian athletes, Christian businessmen. So what's the matter with being a Christian gangster? If I have to give up all that—if that's Christianity—count me out."[8]

The contrast between Jim Vaus and Mickey Cohen illustrates exactly what the apostle James writes about in this passage. Both Vaus and Cohen made a profession of faith under the evangelistic ministry of Billy Graham. Jim Vaus understood that by receiving Jesus as Savior he was also receiving Jesus as the Lord of his life. He literally sold everything he had in order to follow Jesus. He turned his life upside down to follow Jesus. He became a changed man to follow Jesus.

Mickey Cohen, on the other hand, thought he could receive Jesus as his Savior without submitting to Jesus as his Lord. It made perfect sense to him that a Christian could be a gangster. And when he found out that he couldn't be both a Christian and a gangster, he chose to remain a gangster. He had made a profession of faith, but his faith was never real, and his works proved that his faith was dead. In both cases, the issue was faith, not works. The faith of Jim Vaus was proven by his works. The supposed faith of Mickey Cohen was proven false by his actions. Works couldn't save either man, but works proved which man's faith was real.

We know there is no conflict between the apostle Paul and the apostle James because Paul made a practically identical argument in his letter to the Ephesians: "For we are his workmanship, created in Christ Jesus for good works, which God prepared beforehand, that we should walk in them" (Ephesians 2:10).

Here is the point that both James and Paul are making: We are not saved *through* good works or *by* good works. We are saved *for* good works. Our good works will never save us, but our good works are evidence that we have been saved. Our good works will never save us, but God saved us so that we would do good works in his name.

We have to ask ourselves, "If every Christian in the world were just like me, doing the works I do, living the lifestyle I live, would the work of the church get done? Would there be any evangelism? Would the widows and orphans be cared for? Would there be any outreach to the poor, to the outcasts, to the prisoners?"

The moment you came to Christ, God had work for you to do. He had good works waiting for you to accomplish. Are you doing them? Are you carrying out the ministry God designed for your life?

Four reasons why counterfeit faith can't save us

James writes in 2:17, "So also faith by itself, if it does not have works, is dead." The reformed theologian John Calvin observed, "It is faith alone that justifies, but faith that justifies can never be alone." Or as Bible teacher Warren Wiersbe once put it, "We are not saved by faith plus good works, but by a faith that works." Faith can never be by itself; authentic faith produces good works of righteousness.

A person with only an intellectual experience of faith has a faith that is dead. In his mind, this person knows the doctrine of salvation, but in his life, he has never submitted to it. There are thousands, if not millions, who call themselves Christians but have nothing to show for it. They can articulate Christian doctrine, but those doctrines have never touched their hearts or moved their hands. Their profession of faith is worthless.

Dead faith can talk the talk, but it cannot walk the walk. The lips move, but the feet don't stir from a place of indifference. Dead faith professes to believe in Christ, yet attempts nothing for his sake. Beware of those who can talk about faith yet their lives do not match their talk. As the apostle John wrote, "Whoever has the Son has life; whoever does not have the Son of God does not have life" (1 John 5:12).

A dead faith, a faith that has no works and has no life, is truly a counterfeit faith. It lulls you into a false confidence of eternal life. So we have to ask ourselves: *Is my faith real? Is it alive? Is there evidence, in the form of good works, to prove that I have a genuine faith?*

Religiosity can't get you into heaven. Churchianity can't get you into heaven. Only a genuine, living faith in Jesus Christ as your Lord and Savior can carry you through this life and safely into the next. Only an utter surrender to him can get you into heaven.

Counterfeit faith may rely on tradition or denomination: "I was raised in the Such-and-Such Tradition or the So-and-So Denomination, and that's how I know I'm saved." Counterfeit faith may rely on a set of rules: "I don't drink or smoke or play cards or go to dances, so I know I'm saved." Whatever we base our faith on, if it is anything other than faith in Jesus Christ as our Lord and Savior, it is a dead faith, a counterfeit faith. James gives us four reasons why a counterfeit faith cannot save us:

First, *counterfeit faith has no power to save.* "What good is it, my brothers," James wrote, "if someone says he has faith but does not have works? Can that faith save him?" (2:14). If so-called faith does not produce a radical change, it doesn't deserve to be called faith. In John 3, we meet Nicodemus, a Pharisee, a deeply religious man. Nicodemus comes to Jesus by night, professing to believe in Jesus. "No one can do the things you do," Nicodemus tells him, "unless God is with him." But Jesus makes it clear to Nicodemus that true faith involves a radical change—a change so complete and profound that Jesus refers to it as being "born again." A faith that does not change a person from top to bottom is false and has no power to save.

Second, *counterfeit faith is worthless because it doesn't serve others.* When we are self-centered and self-absorbed, we can't see the needs of other people around us. "If a brother or sister is poorly clothed and lacking in daily food," James writes, "and one of you says to them, 'Go in peace, be warmed and filled,' without giving them the things needed for the body, what good is that?" (2:15-16). Genuine Christians have a Christlike concern for others; people of counterfeit faith are concerned only with themselves.

Third, *counterfeit faith is worthless because it offers no evidence of its reality.* James writes, "But someone will say, 'You have faith and I have works.' Show me your faith apart from your works, and I will show you my faith by my works" (2:18). As Christians, it's our job to serve as examples and exhibits of God's saving grace. If the lives we live do not exemplify God's grace, we offer no evidence to the world that the gospel of Jesus Christ is true. If we claim to have faith in Jesus Christ but our lives show no evidence that Jesus lives through us, our faith is worthless and dead—and there is a distinct possibility that we have never experienced saving faith.

Fourth, James makes a truly shocking claim: *counterfeit faith is worthless because it is the same faith that Satan and his demons have!* James writes, "You believe that God is one; you do well. Even the demons believe—and shudder!" (2:19). James wants to shock us into the realization that the Christian faith is much more than simply agreeing with certain doctrines and creeds. Satan agrees with biblical doctrine. He knows better than any human being that Jesus is the only begotten Son of God the Father, that Jesus was crucified, that he suffered and died, and that he rose again on the third day. But knowing these truths doesn't make Satan a Christian.

Does it shock you to realize that demons have faith? Does it amaze you to realize that there are no atheist or agnostic demons? The demons believe 100 percent, without the least particle of doubt, that Jesus is the promised Messiah, born of a virgin, fully God and fully man. Whenever demons encountered Jesus during his earthly ministry, they testified to who he was (see Matthew 3:11 and Luke 8:31).

James wants us to know that many Christians practice a satanic, demonic faith. Like the demons, we believe one way and live another. We profess ourselves to be Christians—but by our speech, our actions, and our way of life, we prove our faith to be counterfeit. We believe that Jesus is the Son of God and that he died on the cross to save us. Big deal! The demons believe all of that, and they at least have the good sense to shudder in terror of God's judgment. We are blithely unconcerned about the way we abuse his mercy and grace.

It is a dangerous thing to practice a counterfeit faith. James warns us against becoming lulled into a false sense of security and complacency. It's a warning that everyone who claims to be a Christian should soberly consider and heed.

Examples of faith—the patriarch and the prostitute

A counterfeit faith is a dead faith. It has no more excitement than a dead romance, no more feeling than a dead nerve, no more power than a dead engine, and no more life than a dead body. A counterfeit faith can only deceive you and leave you empty.

But genuine, authentic faith in Jesus as your only Savior and Lord is an active, dynamic, living faith. A counterfeit faith affects only your intellect, but a genuine, authentic faith in Jesus Christ involves the will, the emotions, the spirit, the soul—indeed, every aspect of your life. Your entire being will come alive with a saving and dynamic faith. Your mind will comprehend the truth. Your heart will desire the truth. Your soul will act on the truth. Your spirit will embody the truth.

How can you tell the difference between a dead counterfeit faith and a dynamic and saving faith? James tells us in the concluding verses of this chapter:

> Do you want to be shown, you foolish person, that faith apart from works is useless? Was not Abraham our father justified by works when he offered up his son Isaac on the altar? You see that faith was active along with his works, and faith was completed by his works; and the Scripture was fulfilled that says, "Abraham believed God, and it was counted to him as righteousness"—and he was called a friend of God. You see that a person is justified by works and not by faith alone. And in the same way was not also Rahab the prostitute justified by works when she received the messengers and sent them out by another way? For as the body apart from the spirit is dead, so also faith apart from works is dead (2:20-26).

When faith is genuine, your claim matches your conduct. Your walk matches your talk. Sincerity is proven by its action. Belief is transformed into commitment. Love is transformed into obedience. Genuine faith cannot accept Jesus as Savior while rejecting him as Lord. Genuine faith denies the self, moves mountains, knows answered prayer, loves others, and continually seeks to please the Lord.

James offers two examples of such faith, Abraham and Rahab. This is a fascinating pairing of Old Testament examples. You could not choose two more contrasting examples than Abraham and Rahab. They were on opposite sides of the cultural fence, the religious fence, the economic fence, and the moral fence. One was an honored patriarch of the Jewish people; the other a despised Gentile prostitute.

But both had one thing in common: a living, dynamic faith—a faith that was demonstrated by risky, courageous action. Both Abraham and Rahab trusted God to an extreme limit, and both acted upon their faith in a dynamic way. Their walk matched their talk. Their claims matched their conduct.

Some people stumble over verse 21: "Was not Abraham our father justified by works when he offered up his son Isaac on the altar?" Is James saying that Abraham was saved by his act of offering Isaac? Of course not. Read Paul's commentary on the story of Abraham in Romans 4, where he writes, "For if Abraham was justified by works, he has something to boast about, but not before God. For what does the Scripture say? 'Abraham believed God, and it was counted to him as righteousness'" (Romans 4:2-3; Paul quotes Genesis 15:6).

Genesis states, and Paul agrees, that Abraham was justified by faith. And James also agrees, but in keeping with his theme throughout this chapter, he places an emphasis on the importance of works as the evidence and outworking of faith. James knows that it was Abraham's faith, not his works, that God counted as righteousness. But James wants us to know exactly what kind of faith Abraham had—a faith that was proven by action, a breathtakingly dynamic and vibrant faith that astonishes us with its bold, unquestioning obedience.

There is no contradiction between Genesis 15, Romans 4, and James 2. The principle of faith is clearly declared in Genesis and Romans, and James expands on this principle by explaining to us, through the actions of Abraham, the dynamic nature of Abraham's faith. Genuine faith obeys God and proves itself through bold, obedient action.

The great tragedy of the church today is that all too many church members match the description Paul gave in his letter to Titus:

"They profess to know God, but they deny him by their works. They are detestable, disobedient, unfit for any good work" (Titus 1:16). The second illustration James offers is that of Rahab the prostitute, whose story is recorded in Joshua chapters 2 and 6. Joshua sent spies into the Promised Land in advance of his planned invasion. Rahab, who lived in the doomed city of Jericho, received and protected the Hebrew spies. She believed the message of doom that Joshua's men preached, and she proved her faith by her actions. She risked her life in carrying out her faith in God. Because of her great faith, she was chosen by God to become an ancestor of our Lord. Rahab grasped the truth and acted on it, exhibiting the kind of genuine faith that was proven by action.

James concludes with a powerful statement: "For as the body apart from the spirit is dead, so also faith apart from works is dead" (2:26). What is a human body worth once the spirit has departed? Nothing! It is a mere corpse, fit only to be buried before corruption sets in. So it is with a faith that has no outward manifestation.

The only faith worthy of the name is a faith that changes lives and goes to work for God, boldly doing his will. How do you acquire such a dynamic, active faith? You can receive it only as a gift from God.

During the Spanish-American war, Clara Barton, the founder of the Red Cross, was ministering to the wounded in Cuba. One day, Colonel Theodore Roosevelt came to her and offered to buy food for some of his sick and wounded Rough Riders.

"No," she replied. "I won't sell it to you."

Roosevelt argued with her, but she steadfastly refused to sell him the supplies. Angry and frustrated, unable to understand her refusal, Roosevelt went to the surgeon in charge and complained to him about this unreasonable woman.

The surgeon was amused. "Colonel," he said, "just *ask* for the supplies."

A smile spread across Roosevelt's face. In an instant, he understood his error. He had been trying to buy the provisions, but the provisions were not for sale.

He went back to Clara Barton and humbly asked for the provisions.

She gave them to him, graciously and without charge.

You cannot purchase saving faith. You cannot buy your way into heaven. Many people have tried, and they go away frustrated. Paradoxically, all you have to do is ask. Simply call upon the name of the Lord, and you will receive saving faith as a free gift of his grace.

And once you have saving faith, you will prove it by the life you lead. You won't be able to help it. You'll just want to serve God and serve others out of gratitude for this free gift you have received.

Have you received the gift of saving faith? If not, will you ask for it today?

6

The Power of the Tongue

obert "R. G." LeTourneau was an inventor and businessman who designed and sold large earthmoving equipment. His company produced everything from construction equipment to oil drilling platforms to missile launchers. He was a devout Christian and the founder of LeTourneau University in Texas. By the time of his death, he was giving 90 percent of his income to the Lord's work while living on the remaining 10 percent. He once said, "The question is not how much of my money I give to God, but rather how much of God's money I keep for myself."

LeTourneau tells the story of one particular model of earthmoving equipment. "We used to have a scraper known as the Model G. Somebody asked one of our salesmen what the 'G' stood for. The salesman was pretty quick on the trigger and replied, 'Well, I guess the G stands for gossip, because like gossip, this machine moves a lot of dirt, and moves it fast!"[9]

The destructive power of gossip was one of the issues on the mind of James when he wrote James 3. This chapter deals with one of the most important steps toward Christian maturity, the control of the tongue. Why is it so important for us, as Christians, to tame the tongue? Our tongues have the power to wound feelings, devastate reputations, shatter self-esteem, and destroy relationships. An uncontrolled tongue can ruin your witness for Christ and bring discredit to Jesus and his gospel. James deals with the issue of the tongue with characteristic bluntness:

> Not many of you should become teachers, my brothers, for you know that we who teach will be judged with greater strictness. For we all stumble in many ways. And if anyone does not stumble in what he says, he is a perfect man, able also to bridle his whole body. If we put bits into the mouths of horses so that they obey us, we guide their whole bodies as well. Look at the ships also: though they are so large and are driven by strong winds, they are guided by a very small rudder wherever the will of the pilot directs. So also the tongue is a small member, yet it boasts of great things (3:1-5a).

James begins by addressing the self-appointed know-it-alls in the church—those who crave attention, who love the limelight, and who want to be considered wise and knowledgeable and spiritual. When James writes, "Not many of you should become teachers," he is saying, "Stop and think before you leap into a position of teaching and leadership, because leaders and teachers will be judged by God according to a much stricter standard."

Godly ambition versus ungodly ambition

The Bible commends those who have zeal and a holy ambition to serve God—servants like Joshua with his passion for conquering the Promised Land, Gideon with his zeal to save Israel, Jeremiah with his goal of restoring the kingdom, and Paul with his zeal for preaching the gospel and propagating the church. But the Scriptures are also filled with stories of those who sought prominence for the sake of personal gain.

In Numbers 12, Miriam and Aaron were overcome with ambition and resentment toward Moses and tried to usurp his leadership role. Because they selfishly opposed the divinely appointed leader, God afflicted Miriam with leprosy.

And in 2 Kings 5, Gehazi, the greedy assistant of the prophet Elisha, coveted the gifts of silver and clothing that Naaman the Syrian leper had brought for Elisha. Gehazi obtained the gifts through dishonesty, and Elisha denounced Gehazi's crime and pronounced a punishment: The leprosy of Naaman would now afflict Gehazi and his family.

In 2 Samuel 14 through 18, we learn the story of Absalom, the self-seeking third son of King David, who revolted against his father, drove him into exile, and was killed in battle in the forest of Ephraim.

Matthew 20 tells us of the mother of James and John, the sons of Zebedee, who was ambitious for her sons and went secretly to Jesus, asking him to appoint them to the top leadership positions in his kingdom.

In Acts 5, we encounter the story of Ananias and Sapphira, members of the early church in Jerusalem. This couple sold a plot of land and donated a portion of the proceeds to the church—but when they presented the donation to Peter, they claimed they were giving all. Because they lied, not just to Peter but to the Holy Spirit, Ananias and Sapphira died on the spot.

And in Acts 8, we meet Simon the magician, who believed in Christ and was baptized—but then wanted to purchase from the apostles the power to perform miracles. But Peter replied, "May your silver perish with you, because you thought you could obtain the gift of God with money! You have neither part nor lot in this matter, for your heart is not right before God" (Acts 8:20-21).

Unfortunately, selfish ambition is all too common among God's people. Many follow the pattern of Simon the magician. He received Christ with sincerity, but then greed, lust for power, and lust for fame took hold. Like Simon, people sometimes see the church and the Christian faith as a way to exalt themselves instead of bringing glory to God. We need to constantly purify our ambitions to make sure that our desire is to serve the Lord Jesus, not our own selfish lusts. As James warns us, "Not many of you should become teachers, my brothers, for you know that we who teach will be judged with greater strictness. For we all stumble in many ways" (3:1-2).

This is a message we should all take seriously and soberly. James is not telling us that it is wrong to want to lead in the church. Far from it! He is saying that we should search ourselves and make sure our motives are pure before we seek a position of leadership. We should make sure that our ambition is to serve God and serve others, not serve ourselves. We should make sure that our goal is to seek the lost, not to seek our own gain.

Do you aspire to leadership in the church? If so, then learn the process of biblical correction, not crude and harmful criticism. Learn biblical discipline, not domination. Learn biblical authority, not autocracy. Learn how to lead, not how to lord it over others. James is warning against fleshly ambition and critical attitudes—and humbly includes himself in this warning, saying, "we who teach will be judged."

Whenever I stand in the pulpit, or sit in a radio or television studio, or contemplate writing a book, I am overwhelmed with the awesome responsibility of interpreting the Word of God. I know that any time I shoulder the task of teaching God's Word, I invite a special measure of God's scrutiny on my life, my thoughts, my actions, and my words. I never begin the task without asking God to take complete control of my words. For every hour I preach or teach, I spend about twenty to thirty hours in preparation, prayer, study, and research.

We who teach will be judged, and that truth should make us

think very seriously about what we are teaching others through the words we speak and the lives we lead.

The creative and destructive power of words

Whether you hold a formal position as a teacher, preacher, or leader in the church, or you're a volunteer Sunday school teacher or Bible study leader, or you're an everyday Christian seeking to live out your faith in your workplace, campus, military unit, or neighborhood—you are involved in teaching. You are setting an example and demonstrating the truth of the gospel, with or without words. You are teaching your spouse, your children, your neighbors, your friends, your students, your teachers, your coworkers, your boss, your teammates.

That's why James goes on to say that it's important for us to watch what we say. And here, he doesn't just address those who are in formal leadership or teaching positions. He addresses all Christians because all of us shall render an account for the words we speak in the day of judgment: "For we all stumble in many ways. And if anyone does not stumble in what he says, he is a perfect man, able also to bridle his whole body" (3:2).

Isn't that true? We are all prone to stumble in various ways. Some of us have a problem controlling our appetites, some of us are lazy and unmotivated, some of us have a problem controlling our emotions, some of us have a problem with tobacco or alcohol or some other substance. We all stumble in different ways. But the person who is able to control the tongue, who is self-disciplined in speech, tends to be more self-controlled in other areas of life as well.

Jesus said, "for by your words you will be justified, and by your words you will be condemned" (Matthew 12:37). If you confess with your tongue that Jesus Christ is Lord of your life, then you will be saved and justified by those words.

A man once said to me, "All this Jesus stuff is just not for me." To him it was a casual, off-the-cuff statement. But I have to tell you, my blood froze when I heard him say that. If you say those words, you are already condemned by those words. No one else condemns you. God does not condemn you. Your own tongue has condemned you.

This doesn't mean that person is beyond the reach of God's grace. If he repents of those words, repents of his sins, and confesses with his tongue that Jesus Christ is Lord, he will be saved. But as long as he stands by his words, he is condemned by his own tongue.

God places a high premium on words. In Genesis 1, God speaks—and the world comes into existence. In John 1:1, John describes Jesus, the Son of God, in this way: "In the beginning was the Word, and the Word was with God, and the Word was God." So God does not take words lightly.

What you and I say with our mouths is vitally and eternally important. That is why the psalmist writes:

> Set a guard, O LORD, over my mouth;
>   keep watch over the door of my lips!
>   (Psalm 141:3)

This is powerful imagery. The psalmist pictures our face as a fortress, and he describes the mouth as the door to that fortress. He asks God to set an armed guard in front of the door to keep watch so that nothing evil would pass through the door.

In the same way, James wants us to understand the power of the tongue. He uses different metaphors than the psalmist uses, but he makes a similar point when he tells us, "If we put bits into the mouths of horses so that they obey us, we guide their whole bodies as well. Look at the ships also: though they are so large and are driven by strong winds, they are guided by a very small rudder wherever the will of the pilot directs. So also the tongue is a small member, yet it boasts of great things" (3:3-5).

James's logic is compelling. These small objects—the bit, the rudder, and the tongue—are very much alike. They are control devices that affect the course of much larger objects. The bit in the horse's mouth, the rudder that steers the ship, and the tongue that wags in our mouths—these are such small objects, yet they wield such incredible power and produce such profound effects.

The same mouth, the same tongue, can yield wildly different results, depending on the words we choose to speak. And our words depend on the condition of our hearts. As we read in Proverbs,

> The mouth of the righteous is a fountain of life,
>   but the mouth of the wicked conceals violence.
> (Proverbs 10:11)

Our lips can produce words of love, comfort, blessing, encouragement, wisdom, and inspiration. Our lips can send forth a message of faith that can lead people to Christ and forever alter their eternal destinies.

Yet those same lips can also produce words of hate, sarcasm, condemnation, cursing, affliction, accusation, and bitterness. Our lips can spread lies and rumors. Our lips can so embitter people that they will determine never to listen to the gospel again for as long as they live.

Mary, Queen of Scots, once said she feared the tongue of the Scottish Protestant reformer John Knox more than ten thousand fighting men. Why? Because John Knox preached the truth. A tongue that speaks the truth is a powerful force for good—and for God. But a tongue that disregards the truth can be a powerful force for destruction.

There's an old saying, "The Christian army is the only army that shoots its wounded." It's a sad statement, and all too true. How do we shoot each other? With the weapon of the tongue.

A brother or sister in Christ suffers an illness, an injury, or the loss of a loved one—and some thoughtless, unfeeling church member goes to them and says, "You know why this happened to you? There must be unconfessed sin in your life. God is punishing you, and you need to repent of that sin." That's called shooting the wounded.

Or we receive word that fellow Christians are divorcing, or are involved in a scandal, or their unwed daughter is pregnant, or their son is in trouble with the law. We don't know all the facts, and even if we did have all the facts, it wouldn't be any of our business. But the story is just too juicy not to share with others. We may disguise it as a prayer request, but it's nothing but the worst kind of gossip. That's called shooting the wounded.

Many people who would never physically assault anyone would not hesitate to assault the feelings, the relationships, the reputation, or the testimony of a fellow Christian. Many people who would never speak harshly to someone face-to-face will gladly rejoice in private over someone's downfall, saying, "Good! He finally got what he deserved!"

The most common forms of sin in the church are the sins of the tongue. It is so easy to harm one another with the tongue. It takes hardly any effort at all. In fact, most of us find that it takes enormous effort and constant vigilance to *prevent* ourselves from hurting others with our tongues. That's why James wrote, "And if anyone does not stumble in what he says, he is a perfect man, able also to bridle his whole body" (3:2). If you can control your tongue, you can control your entire body.

The spark that ignites the blaze

James goes on to pile metaphor upon metaphor, intensifying this image of the destructive power of the tongue:

> How great a forest is set ablaze by such a small fire! And the tongue is a fire, a world of unrighteousness. The tongue is set among our members, staining the whole body, setting on fire the entire course of life, and set on fire by hell. For every kind of beast and bird, of reptile and sea creature, can be tamed and has been tamed by mankind, but no human being can tame the tongue. It is a restless evil, full of deadly poison. With it we bless our Lord and Father, and with it we curse people who

are made in the likeness of God. From the same mouth come blessing and cursing. My brothers, these things ought not to be so. Does a spring pour forth from the same opening both fresh and salt water? Can a fig tree, my brothers, bear olives, or a grapevine produce figs? Neither can a salt pond yield fresh water (3:5b-12).

Why is it so important that a growing Christian learn to tame his or her tongue? James makes it clear: We must learn to control the tongue because of the tongue's potential for devastation and destruction. Left uncontrolled, the tongue is like a firestorm, torching everything in its path.

When I lived in Australia in the late 1960s, I used to hear the locals talk about a phenomenon called a brushfire. I didn't know anything about brushfires because, coming from the Middle East, I had never seen brushes. But after I had lived in Australia for a few years, we had an especially hot, dry summer—and we had brushfires. I saw with my own eyes the devastating effect of a runaway brushfire. I saw thousands of acres, once fertile and green, turned to ashes. The cause: a cigarette tossed carelessly from the window of a car. Just as that little smoldering cigarette set off a blaze that destroyed thousands of acres, the human tongue can set off a firestorm that destroys lives, reputations, and relationships.

How can the tongue be the spark that ignites a destructive fire? Let me suggest five ways.

First, the tongue ignites a fire through gossip. We tend to excuse our own gossiping and think of gossip as a minor or even harmless vice. But when Paul lists in Romans 1:29 the evil deeds of unrighteous people, he includes gossip alongside malice, strife, deceit, and even murder. And in 1 Timothy 5:13, he warns young Pastor Timothy not to permit the actions of "idlers...gossips and busybodies" to infect the church.

Gossip is a common weakness among many in the church. We love to hear it, and we love to spread it. It makes us feel important to be "in the know." When we have some juicy gossip to share, people pay attention to us and listen to us. It puffs up our ego and our evil pride. We are eager to spread the word, even though we don't know all the details, don't have all the facts, and aren't sure how reliable our information actually is. None of that matters. We don't even care who gets hurt. The only thing that matters is that it's juicy.

One of the most effective ways to neutralize gossip is to stop it in its tracks. Refuse to receive it. A minister was once approached by a few of his parishioners who wanted to report some wrongdoing by a man in the church.

"First, let me ask you a few questions," the pastor said. "Does anyone else know about this matter?"

"No, Pastor."

"You haven't told anyone else?"

"No, Pastor."

"Good. I don't want you to tell me or anyone else about this matter. I want you to go home and pray about it. Lay it at the feet of Jesus. If the Lord leads you to speak directly to this man, then do as the Lord leads. But don't speak to any other person about this unless you go to the man first."

The Lord Jesus gave us a process for dealing with conflicts, wrongdoing, and problems in the church. In Matthew 18:15-20, he tells us that if a Christian brother or sister sins against us, we are to go to that fellow Christian alone and resolve that problem face-to-face. If the fellow Christian listens to us, then we have restored the relationship—"you have gained your brother." If he refuses to listen, we go back to him with one or two other witnesses so that the evidence can be established. If he refuses to listen even to them, then you take the matter to the church for resolution. That's the point at which you involve the church leaders. The vast majority of conflicts and problems in the church could be resolved, and the church would function much more smoothly, if we would obey the wise counsel of our Lord.

Second, the tongue ignites a fire by the utterance of profanity and obscenity. It is hard for me to understand how anyone whose heart is right with God could use foul or lewd language. As the apostle Paul writes, "Let no corrupting talk come out of your mouths, but only such as is good for building up, as fits the occasion, that it may give grace to those who hear...Let there be no filthiness nor foolish talk nor crude joking, which are out of place, but instead let there be thanksgiving" (Ephesians 4:29 and 5:4).

Unwholesome speech corrupts those who speak it and those who hear it. God gave us the power of speech to build one another up and to communicate grace to one another—not as a means of infecting one another with filthy ideas.

Third, the tongue ignites a fire through the utterance of lies and insinuations. The evil tongue of Satan ignited the fire of the Fall by tempting Adam and Eve with lies about the character and promises of God. Many families, marriages, and churches have been destroyed by the spreading of lies and insinuations.

The sin of lying is prohibited by the Ninth Commandment: "You shall not bear false witness against your neighbor" (Exodus 20:16). God is not merely telling us not to give false testimony in a court of law. False witness is any false report, any lie, any insinuation against another person. Elsewhere, God says, "You shall not spread a false report" (Exodus 23:1a). And in the book of Proverbs, Solomon writes:

> There are six things that the LORD hates,
>   seven that are an abomination to him:
> haughty eyes, a lying tongue,
>   and hands that shed innocent blood,
> a heart that devises wicked plans,
>   feet that make haste to run to evil,
> a false witness who breathes out lies,
>   and one who sows discord among brothers.
>   (Proverbs 6:16-19)

In the same book of wisdom, Solomon also tells us,

> Put away from you crooked speech,
> and put devious talk far from you.
> (Proverbs 4:24)

An insinuation or innuendo is an especially perverse form of lying. It's an indirect remark that is intended to suggest something disparaging or derogatory about someone, to plant a destructive idea without coming out and stating the lie plainly. Insinuation has been referred to as "passive-aggressive verbal violence," meaning that an individual tries to hurt other people (that's aggressive) yet without being caught doing so (that's the passive part). Some examples:

"I'm not sure if a person with a past like hers would be comfortable on our committee."

"Oh, I think he'd be an excellent teacher—especially since he's been in recovery."

"I saw a blue Ford parked at the church organist's house yesterday. Does Deacon Smith still drive a blue Ford?"

When you speak, do you build others up with words of grace and truth? Or do you tear others down and stir up dissension with lies and insinuations?

The *way* we speak versus the *words* we speak

Fourth, the tongue ignites a fire by magnifying the faults of others. Many people try to build themselves up by putting others down. They criticize their spouses for not being adequate providers or homemakers. They criticize the pastor for not being an adequate preacher and leader. They criticize their boss or coworkers for being incompetent or stupid.

Always implied in our criticism of others is the unspoken assumption that we could do it better. We put others down to elevate ourselves. Can you imagine Jesus ever putting someone down to make himself look better? If Jesus wouldn't do it, neither should we. The psalmist had this to say about people who use their tongues like swords to cut other people down to size:

> Hide me from the secret plots of the wicked,
>   from the throng of evildoers,
> who whet their tongues like swords,
>   who aim bitter words like arrows,
> shooting from ambush at the blameless,
>   shooting at him suddenly and without fear.
> (Psalm 64:2-4)

The righteous use their tongues to build others up. The wicked use their tongues to cut others down. Whose side are you on when it comes to using your tongue, the side of the righteous—or the side of the wicked?

Fifth, the tongue ignites a fire not only by the words it speaks but by the way it speaks those words. Our tone of voice can either intensify and underline our words or cancel out their meaning altogether. Suppose you and I were to meet, and I looked you in the eye, smiled at you, and energetically said, "It's nice to meet you!" You would receive the message that I was genuinely pleased to be in your presence. But suppose I said those exact same words, but I said them with a flat, expressionless tone, a sour expression, and without even looking up from a magazine I was reading. Would you get the same message that I was pleased to be in your presence? Of course not. Yet I used exactly the same words both times—same words, different meaning.

When we speak to each other, our tone and other nonverbal cues (facial expression, eye contact, gestures, and body language) are a major factor in either amplifying the meaning of our words or negating that meaning. As the philosopher Friedrich Nietzsche once observed, "We often refuse to accept an idea merely because the tone of voice in which it has been expressed is unsympathetic to us."

Humorist and publisher Bennett Cerf told a story (which he purported to be true) of a European immigrant who came to America planning to make his fortune and then send money back to his wife in the old country so she could join him. The immigrant began working in the theater district in New York City. He quickly prospered, though he was unable to read and write. He was having such a good time and making such good money that he forgot all about his wife and his promise to send money to her.

After six months, the immigrant received a letter from his wife. Being illiterate, he asked a friend to read the letter to him. His friend was a gruff, unfriendly man who bellowed like a foghorn. He read the wife's words in an angry, gravelly tone: "Why haven't you sent for me? I must have some money right away. Minnie."

The immigrant snatched the letter and stuffed it in his pocket. Angered by the demanding attitude he heard in his wife's words, he no longer wanted to bring her to America.

About a month later, the immigrant found himself standing next to a noted playwright, a soft-spoken man with a refined manner of speaking. The immigrant took the letter out of his pocket and asked the playwright, "Will you read my wife's letter to me please?"

The playwright agreed. He took the letter, and in a gentle, almost wistful voice, read, "Why haven't you sent for me? I must have some money right away. Minnie."

"Well," the immigrant said, "I'm glad to hear that she changed her tone!"[10]

It was the same letter, but the man heard two different messages because the words were spoken in different tones. The *way* we speak is just as important as the *words* we speak.

How to tame the tongue

"The tongue," James writes, "is set among our members, staining the whole body, setting on fire the entire course of life, and set on fire by hell" (3:6). That is a dire description of the tongue and the destruction it causes. What is the solution? Can't we simply *choose* to control our tongues? Can't we, through sheer willpower, put an end to our bad habits of gossiping, swearing, lying, faultfinding, and causing hurt and division in our families and churches?

James replies: No, we can't. He explains, "For every kind of beast and bird, of reptile and sea creature, can be tamed and has been tamed by mankind, but no human being can tame the tongue. It is a restless evil, full of deadly poison" (3:7-8). James tells us that it is easier to tame wild beasts then to tame the tongue. The untamed tongue is a stark symbol of our human inability to live and speak and act as we know we should. As Paul writes, "For I do not do the good I want, but the evil I do not want is what I keep on doing" (Romans 7:19).

We can send robotic spaceships to Mars and control their actions from millions of miles away. We can build a dam on a mighty river and control the water's flow and harness its energy to light our homes. We are learning how to control and eradicate diseases that have plagued the human race for thousands of years.

But we have never learned how to control the human heart. We have never learned how to tame the human tongue. As a result, our actions and words are divided. One moment, the tongue is praising God and serving others. The next moment, the same tongue is doing evil. As James explains, "With it [the tongue] we bless our Lord and Father, and with it we curse people who are made in the likeness of God. From the same mouth come blessing and cursing. My brothers, these things ought not to be so" (3:9-10).

This conclusion leads James to ask a series of rhetorical questions: "Does a spring pour forth from the same opening both fresh and salt water? Can a fig tree, my brothers, bear olives, or a grapevine produce figs? Neither can a salt pond yield fresh water" (3:11-12). The same tongue cannot be an instrument of both blessing and cursing, just as salt water and fresh water cannot flow from the same spring.

Christians cannot simply come to church on Sunday, sing praises to God, then go throughout the week cursing, lying, gossiping, criticizing, arguing, yelling, and berating others. If our tongue is not brought under control, evil and sin will gain the upper hand. Cursing and gossiping will become the reality of our lives, and the blessing that we do will be all for show, a hypocritical act.

That's why James concludes, "My brothers, these things ought not to be so" (3:10).

You and I are powerless to tame the tongue, to control the critical spirit, to calm the angry heart. But that doesn't mean we have no hope. What we cannot do in our own strength, God's Holy Spirit can do through the power of the cleansing blood of Christ. We can do all things through Christ who strengthens us, and God stands ready to live his life through us, to take control of our tongues, to cleanse us and set us free.

If we will go to him and with our tongues confess our sins to him and our faith in him, then he will come in and take control of our tongues. Every morning when we start the day, and hourly as we go through the day, we can say, "Lord, I give you my tongue. Sanctify it, control it, and use it to reach others with the good news of Jesus Christ. Give me your words of grace and love to speak today. And I will bless you with my tongue throughout all the days of my life."

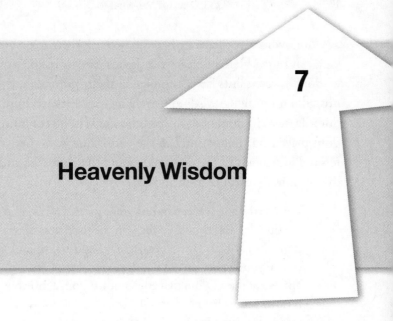

Heavenly Wisdom

The story is told of a young man who lent five hundred dollars to a friend. Unfortunately, he failed to get an IOU from the friend and had nothing in writing to prove he had lent the money. More than a year had gone by, and the friend made no effort to repay the loan. This young man wanted his money, and he knew he needed some wise advice on how to motivate his friend to repay the loan. So he went to his father, told him the story, and said, "What should I do?"

"The solution is really quite simple, Son," his father said. "Write your friend a note and tell him you need him to repay the thousand dollars he owes you."

"No, Dad. It's five hundred dollars."

"Son, you need to say 'one thousand dollars.' He'll write back and tell you he only owes you five hundred—and then you'll have it in writing."

And that son knew he had come to the right place for wisdom.

In chapter 1, James wrote, "If any of you lacks wisdom, let him ask God, who gives generously to all without reproach, and it will be given him." Here in chapter 3, James returns to the subject of wisdom. Many saints have stumbled in their spiritual journey and missed out on divine wisdom by relying on their own human wisdom. James had undoubtedly seen the tragic results of human wisdom played out many times in the early church. So he writes to remind his readers of the need to conduct themselves according to the wisdom that comes from above:

> Who is wise and understanding among you? By his good conduct let him show his works in the meekness of wisdom. But if you have bitter jealousy and selfish ambition in your hearts, do not boast and be false to the truth. This is not the wisdom that comes down from above, but is earthly, unspiritual, demonic. For where jealousy and selfish ambition exist, there will be disorder and every vile practice. But the wisdom from above is first pure, then peaceable, gentle, open to reason, full of mercy and good fruits, impartial and sincere. And a harvest of righteousness is sown in peace by those who make peace (3:13-18).

Wisdom is shown by its actions. If anyone claims to be wise, let him prove it by the way he lives his life. God isn't interested in empty words or meaningless gestures. His goal is to produce a society of people who back up their words with action. Head knowledge is useless if genuine godly wisdom does not produce a godly lifestyle within us.

Jealousy and selfish ambition

You don't need a university degree to be wise. You don't need a genius IQ to be wise. You don't need to be a rocket scientist or a brain surgeon to be wise. Never confuse wisdom with intelligence or education. Many highly educated people have no wisdom to speak of. And many people with very little knowledge or education have great depths of wisdom that they put to good use every day.

Knowledge enables us to take things apart; wisdom enables us to put things back together. Knowledge tells us how to build an atomic bomb; wisdom tells us how to keep those bombs from being launched in anger. Knowledge tells us how to build a computer; wisdom tells us how to use that computer for good instead of evil. Knowledge tells us how to do it; wisdom tells us what we ought to do and why.

God intends for his people to immerse themselves in his wisdom and to live out his wisdom in their everyday lives. You can draw a straight line from James's statement at the beginning of chapter 3 ("Not many of you should become teachers, my brothers") to his statement in verse 13 ("Who is wise and understanding among you? By his good conduct let him show his works in the meekness of wisdom"). James seeks to weed out those who have selfish ambition for prominence in the church and to encourage those whose only ambition is for God's true wisdom, which is demonstrated in meekness, not pride.

The Bible demonstrates again and again that godly wisdom means being God-centered instead of self-centered. We tend to be occupied with the self, concerned with our reputation, and protective of our ego and image. But God wants us to be occupied with him, concerned with glorifying him, and eager to advance his reputation and his message in our generation.

In all the turmoil of today's world, in all the pressures and responsibilities we face at home and in the workplace, in all the strains and stresses in our relationships, these three truths stand firm:

1. God is the Creator, so he stands at the beginning of all things.

2. God is faithful, so he stands in the center of things.

3. God is the judge, so he stands at the end of things.

When you truly grasp these three truths, you will have the wisdom to wait on God, trusting that his plan and his timetable are always best for you.

Can a Christian run his or her life according to Satan's "wisdom"? Unfortunately, the answer is yes! When we abandon God's wisdom, we inevitably become ensnared by Satan's false wisdom. James writes, "But if you have bitter jealousy and selfish ambition in your hearts, do not boast and be false to the truth. This is not the wisdom that comes down from above, but is earthly, unspiritual, demonic. For where jealousy and selfish ambition exist, there will be disorder and every vile practice" (3:14-16).

Though James is speaking to teachers whose hearts are not focused on things of the Lord, his words apply to all believers. His reasoning is simple: When our hearts are filled with "jealousy and selfish ambition," our judgment is impaired. Bitterness, jealousy, and selfish ambition blind us to wisdom and good judgment. Jealous, ambitious people are unreliable. They can't be objective. Their words and actions are colored by self-centered motives and clouded by bitter emotions.

Jealousy and selfish ambition produce untold tragedy and dysfunction in the church. Bitterness, jealousy, and selfish ambitions arise from a world system that is controlled by Satan and his false wisdom. Satanic wisdom that is "earthly, unspiritual, demonic" has a limited range of vision—it sees only this world. It promotes corrupt values of selfishness, greed, and lust. It cares only about the here and now, ignoring eternity. Satanic wisdom is the lie that tells us we can control our own destiny and become our own gods.

Bitter jealousy is frequently caused by a belief that we are being used or abused by other people. When a wife believes she is taken for granted by her husband, she feels bitter and resentful. When an employee believes he is exploited and treated as a slave by the boss, he becomes bitter and resentful. When children believe they are abused or neglected or mistreated by parents, they grow up feeling bitter and resentful.

The solution we need is to replace the satanic wisdom of jealousy, selfishness, and resentment with the meek and humble wisdom of God.

The false wisdom of this world

The famed British dramatist Fredrick Lonsdale was celebrating New Year's Eve at London's Garrick Club when he was approached by a fellow playwright, Sir Arthur Seymour Hicks. Pointing to another man across the room, a fellow member of the club, Hicks suggested to Lonsdale that the close of the old year and the beginning of the new was a good time to patch up differences. Lonsdale had clashed and quarreled many times with the man across the room and had stubbornly resisted restoring their friendship. "Why don't you go over now and wish him a happy New Year?" Hicks said. Lonsdale agreed to do so. He crossed the room and tapped his foe on the shoulder. Then Lonsdale told the man, "I wish you a happy New Year—but only one."[11]

Bitter jealousy produces the deadly poison of resentment in the lives of those who live according to the wisdom of this world, a wisdom that James calls "earthly, unspiritual, demonic."

And what about selfish ambition? James writes, "But if you have bitter jealousy and selfish ambition in your hearts, do not boast and be false to the truth" (3:14). Selfish ambition clouds our judgment and taints our motives. We easily fool ourselves into thinking we are ambitious to serve God, when in reality we are ambitious for praise, position, and recognition in the church. We are ambitious to be thought of as devoted, saintly, and godly when in reality, all of our religious works are just for show, intended to impress others.

Selfish ambition has wrecked many marriages, families, and churches. People who are motivated by selfish ambition are not motivated by Christlike love. Without love, marriages and families and churches die—and it is selfish ambition that nails the coffin shut. Selfish ambition causes strife and competition. People who are selfishly ambitious can never rest, can never know peace. There is always someone else to envy, someone else to compete with.

Those who are driven by selfish ambition go from job to job, from one relationship to the next, from one church to another. They are never happy. They never know peace. They are consumed with jealousy. They are driven to work harder and achieve more in order to keep up appearances. Their unholy restlessness and envy eats them up inside.

Selfish ambition caused the fall of Satan. Selfish ambition and jealousy led Cain to murder his brother, Abel. Selfish ambition and jealousy led the sons of Jacob to sell their brother, Joseph, into slavery. Selfish ambition moved Korah to rebel against the leadership of Moses, leading to the destruction of Korah and his coconspirators. Selfish ambition gripped the heart of Absalom and compelled him to rebel against his father, King David. Selfish ambition prompted Haman to plot against Queen Esther's kinsman Mordecai—and the gallows Haman planned for Mordecai became the instrument of his own death. Selfish ambition drove the religious leaders to conspire against Jesus and deliver him to Pontius Pilate.

No wonder the apostle Paul tells us, "Do all things without grumbling or disputing, that you may be blameless and innocent, children of God without blemish in the midst of a crooked and twisted generation, among whom you shine as lights in the world" (Philippians 2:14-15). There is no limit to the sins that proceed from a heart filled with jealousy and selfish ambition.

The tarnished, deceptive wisdom that inspires jealousy and selfishness in our hearts does not come from God, James says. Such false wisdom is earthly, unspiritual, and demonic. It is earthly because it is a product of the world's system—a system that is ruled by "the god of this world" (as Paul calls Satan in 2 Corinthians 4:4). It is unspiritual because it does not come from the Holy Spirit. It is demonic because it is of the devil, and it always leads to division, destruction, and defeat. Satan is the source of this wisdom, and he delights in inflicting the evil consequences of this false wisdom on the human race.

If you are a believer and you are being eaten up with bitter jealousy or consumed with selfish ambition, I urge you to deal with it today, right now, before you even turn this page. Do not let Satan get his hooks into you. Repent of it. Ask the Spirit to fill you and purge you of this poison before it destroys you.

What happens when you use worldly wisdom to accomplish God's work? The end result is always the destruction of the very thing you want to achieve. You can't do God's work Satan's way. It will come to nothing on earth, and it will lead to nothing in heaven. The wisdom that comes from hell will get you nowhere in heaven.

Eight qualities that come from God's wisdom

Bruce Goodrich graduated from high school with high hopes for his future. He was accepted into the cadet corps at Texas A&M University. As part of the cadet initiation, Bruce and his fellow pledges were sent on a marathon-like forced run at night. During the run, Bruce dropped to the ground—and he didn't get up. The young man was dead before he attended his first college class.

The entire Texas A&M community was stunned and heartbroken by the tragedy. A few days after Bruce's death, the young man's father wrote an open letter to the students, faculty, and cadet corps at the university. Mr. Goodrich wrote, in part:

> I would like to take this opportunity to express the appreciation of my family for the great outpouring of concern and sympathy from Texas A&M University and the college community over the loss of our son Bruce. We were deeply touched by the tribute paid to him in the battalion. We were particularly pleased to note that his Christian witness did not go unnoticed during his brief time on campus.

I hope it will be some comfort to know that we harbor no ill will in the matter. We know our God makes no mistakes. Bruce had an appointment with his Lord and is now secure in his celestial home. When the question is asked, "Why did this happen?" perhaps one answer will be, "So that many will consider where they will spend eternity."[12]

These are the words of a father who is grieving, who is hurting, but who exhibits an amazing wisdom, peace, and mercy. His wisdom is what James calls "the wisdom from above." It is a kind of wisdom that can come only from the heart of an all-wise God. James writes, "But the wisdom from above is first pure, then peaceable, gentle, open to reason, full of mercy and good fruits, impartial and sincere. And a harvest of righteousness is sown in peace by those who make peace" (3:17-18).

James lists eight qualities that are demonstrated in the lives of those who rely on "the wisdom from above." Those eight qualities are purity, peace, gentleness, reasonableness, mercy, fruitfulness, impartiality, and sincerity.

First, let's look at *purity*. James lists purity first because it is the fundamental criterion of all wisdom. Purity is not an outward expression but an inner experience. God examines our hearts before he looks at our hands. Though God is concerned with our deeds, he is even more concerned with who and what we are. After all, it's possible to do all the right things, say all the right words, and go through all the religious motions, and yet do all those things with impure hearts and ungodly motives. We can even preach the gospel, feed the hungry, give to the poor, and visit the prisoners with a selfish motive of winning attention, applause, and praise.

But God always looks on the heart, and he knows if our motive is not right. That's why Jesus said, "Blessed are the pure in heart, for they shall see God" (Matthew 5:8). The heart is the very core of our personality and the source of all of our outward activities. If the heart is impure, all our activities will be tainted. So God is far more interested in the state of our heart than our so-called "good deeds." We see this principle flowing throughout the Old and New Testaments. As the psalmist writes,

> Who shall ascend the hill of the LORD?
> And who shall stand in his holy place?
> He who has clean hands and a pure heart,
>   who does not lift up his soul to what is false
>   and does not swear deceitfully.
> He will receive blessing from the LORD
>   and righteousness from the God of his salvation.
>   (Psalm 24:3-5)

And Solomon wrote,

> Keep your heart with all vigilance,
>   for from it flow the springs of life.
>   (Proverbs 4:23)

The apostle Paul told his spiritual son Timothy, "The aim of our charge is love that issues from a pure heart and a good conscience and a sincere faith" (1 Timothy 1:5). And the apostle Peter wrote, "Love one another earnestly from a pure heart" (1 Peter 1:22b).

The true wisdom that comes from heaven is always characterized by purity of heart. What an extreme contrast there is between the wisdom from heaven and the false wisdom of this world. False wisdom always puts *self* at the center; godly wisdom is undefiled, undivided, and centered on God and is always rooted in purity of heart.

Second, let's look at *peace*. Godly wisdom is always peaceable by nature and produces peace in our hearts. Only when the heart is pure does inner peace become possible. Though we all deal with circumstances from time to time that temporarily disturb our peace, the person who lives with long-term inner turmoil does not know the wisdom that comes from God.

Many people try to baptize false wisdom and make it seem godly. They rationalize their jealousy, bitterness, and selfish ambition, and tell themselves they are only ambitious for God. But their inner turmoil proves them wrong. It shows that they have exchanged God's wisdom for the false wisdom of this world.

James lists peace after purity because purity brings about peace. If you try to achieve peace without a commitment to purity, you will achieve neither peace nor purity. But if you seek purity first, peace will naturally ensue. We can never achieve peace by sweeping our sins under the carpet. Peace is a byproduct of purity.

The false wisdom that comes from Satan tells us to live in denial, to cover up our sin, to focus on an outward hypocritical display while pretending we have no sin. But God's wisdom tells us that if we confess our sins and repent of our sins, we will experience the peace that passes understanding.

Third, let's look at *gentleness*. A good way to define gentleness is "moderation without compromise or weakness." On the 150th birthday of Abraham Lincoln, poet Carl Sandburg stood before a joint session of Congress and gave a speech about Lincoln's character. He said, "Not often in the story of mankind does a man arrive on earth who is both steel and velvet, who is as hard as rock and as soft as drifting fog, who holds in his heart and mind the paradox of terrible storm and peace unspeakable and perfect."[13]

That is an excellent description of what we as Christians should be—people of "steel and velvet…as hard as rock and as soft as drifting fog." We should be people of great gentleness and compassion but absolutely uncompromising when it comes to our Christian principles. That paradoxical quality of gentleness is all too rare in the world, but should be overflowingly abundant in the church of Jesus Christ. It is an essential quality of "the wisdom from above."

Fourth, let's look at *reasonableness*. The "wisdom from above" that James speaks of should make every believer reasonable, rational, agreeable, and easy to get along with. Human wisdom, the source of jealousy and selfish ambition, makes people hard, stubborn, cynical, and unreasonable. But "the wisdom from above" enables God's people to be reasonable and agreeable even in times of disagreement. The worldly wisdom that comes from Satan causes people to rationalize their selfishness. They tell themselves, "I'm not stubborn; I just have strong convictions," or "I'm not unreasonable; I just have high standards," or "I'm not argumentative; I just stand up for what I believe." The wisdom that is "earthly, unspiritual, demonic" makes people unreasonable and disagreeable. It produces division, turmoil, and conflict. But when we live according to God's wisdom, we become good listeners, clear thinkers, and we find that we can stand strong for our convictions and still be understanding of the feelings of others.

Fifth, let's look at *mercy*. James writes, "But the wisdom from above is…full of mercy." The person who relies on God's wisdom is full of mercy and controlled by mercy. This word *mercy* has a double meaning. It means, first, that you possess a spirit of forgiveness toward those who have wronged you; and second, that you are willing and eager to give practical help to those who are in need. As Jesus said, "Be merciful, even as your Father is merciful" (Luke 6:36).

Mercy runs contrary to the human nature. Worldly wisdom says, "Don't get mad, get even!" But godly wisdom, the wisdom from above, says, "Don't get mad. Be merciful. Love your enemies. Do good to those who hate you and hurt you."

Those who live by the wisdom of this fallen world will tell you, "Mercy makes no sense. Forgiving and loving my enemies is unnatural. It runs counter to every fiber of my being." And that's true. The wisdom that comes from heaven is not a natural wisdom. Like the gospel itself, it is *super*natural.

Sixth, let's look at *fruitfulness*. James writes, "But the wisdom from above is…full of mercy and good fruits." A wise, godly Christian produces good fruits and lives a continual lifestyle of fruitfulness. When you live by worldly wisdom, you can't produce the fruit of the Spirit because you are too busy pursuing your own worldly ambition or wallowing in your own jealousy and self-pity. Godly wisdom compels us to bear fruit, to live fruitful lives, to have a sweet and fruitful influence on the lives of everyone around us.

Seventh, let's look at *impartiality*. James writes, "But the wisdom from above is…impartial." The wisdom from God shows no favoritism. Those who live by worldly wisdom cannot be impartial because they are caught up in ambition, in trying to impress others and please others. When you live to impress others, you can never be honest about who you are. You become a chameleon, always changing yourself in order to win acceptance from others, in order to please and impress others. When you are constantly wavering and adjusting your image in order to meet the approval of others, you cannot be impartial. You cannot be your own authentic self. You are constantly being conformed to this or that mold, to meet the expectations of others.

When you live by God's wisdom, however, you no longer live to please others. You live to please God. You are consistent, single-minded, and authentic. You have conviction and purpose. You don't play favorites. You are free to be you.

Eighth, let's look at *sincerity*. James writes, "But the wisdom from above is…sincere." *Sincere* is derived from the Latin *sincerus* which means "pure, sound, whole, and undefiled." As a human attribute, *sincere* literally means "without hypocrisy." A sincere person does not pretend to be something he's not. He is not one sort of person in public and another in private; he is not a Christian on Sunday morning and a pagan on Friday night; he is exactly the same person in every situation. A sincere person never has to hide or wear a mask.

In some Christian circles, people think they have to act the part of a "super Christian." They cannot admit to having flaws or failures. They cannot cry or bleed. They are never vulnerable—and they are never truly honest about who they are. That kind of insincerity does not come from the wisdom of God. It's ungodly wisdom—and it's hypocrisy.

If you are growing in Christ, if you are becoming mature in the wisdom that comes from God, then your life will increasingly demonstrate all eight of these qualities. You won't have to *try* to demonstrate these qualities. God's wisdom will naturally produce them and cause these qualities to flow daily from your life.

The promise of God's wisdom

James concludes his exhortation on the wisdom from above in verse 18: "And a harvest of righteousness is sown in peace by those who make peace." Don't you want to reap a harvest of righteousness? Don't you want to live by the wisdom from above? Don't you want to become one of God's peacemakers?

The wisdom from above can be truly yours! "How?" you ask. You have already received your answer in James 1:5—"If any of you lacks wisdom, let him ask God, who gives generously to all without reproach, and it will be given him." Ask God for wisdom, and he will give it to you, generously and abundantly.

The wisdom from above, the wisdom that comes from God, can be yours if you simply ask God, humble yourself to receive it, and patiently allow God to reveal his will to you. Wisdom doesn't come all at once in a flash, like a lightning strike. It grows within you as you learn to listen to God's voice and follow where he leads.

If you lack wisdom, ask God—and wisdom will be given to you. That is God's promise, and you have his Word on it.

8

Watch Out for the Big Three

I live in Atlanta. Here in the South, the war that most Americans call the Civil War is sometimes called the War of Northern Aggression. One of the great battles of that war, the Battle of Allatoona Pass, was fought on October 5, 1864, in Bartow County, Georgia, not far from Atlanta. A Confederate division under Major General Samuel G. French launched an assault against a heavily fortified Union garrison commanded by Brigadier General John M. Corse. The Union garrison protected the Union supply railroad through Allatoona Pass.

General French's Confederate division began the assault at sunrise with a two-hour artillery bombardment. French finally called a halt to the artillery fire, and he sent the Union commander, General Corse, a demand for surrender. Corse refused. So the Confederate general launched his brigades in a withering two-pronged attack on the Union fortification. The fighting was fierce, the slaughter incredible. It seemed that the Union forces would have no choice but to surrender.

General Corse's force of twenty-one hundred men fought deter-minedly against a vastly superior Confederate force of six thousand troops. During the bloody battle, General Corse lost a third of his men—and he himself sustained head wounds, including a shattered cheekbone and the partial loss of one ear.

A Union officer, Major Daniel Webster Whittle of Massachu-setts, was an eyewitness to these events. He later recorded that the beleaguered Union defenders commanded by General Corse "were slowly driven into a small fort upon the crest of the hill. Many had fallen, and the result seemed to render a prolongation of the fight hopeless."

Just then, when it seemed all hope was lost, one of General Corse's officers saw a signal flag across the valley on the top of Ken-nesaw Mountain. The flag sent a message in semaphore code. The message, Whittle reported, was, "Hold the fort; I am coming. W.T. Sherman." General Corse's own signalman sent back an answer, and soon General William Tecumseh Sherman's words were being waved by semaphore flags from mountaintop to mountaintop.

General Sherman's message of hope pierced the fog of war and enabled General Corse's troops to fight on for another three hours until Sherman's advance guard arrived and forced the Confederates into retreat. A battle that seemed lost was won because the soldiers in the fort now knew that their commander was coming with rein-forcements: "Hold the fort; I am coming."

After the war, Major Whittle became a close associate of evan-gelist Dwight L. Moody. Reflecting on this historic battle, Whittle compared the Battle of Allatoona Pass to the spiritual battles we all face in the Christian life. He wrote, "No incident of the war illus-trates more thrillingly the inspiration imparted by the knowledge of the presence of the Commander…The message of Sherman to the soldiers of Altoona…[reminds us of] the message of the Great Commander [Jesus], who signals ever to all who fight life's battle, 'Hold the fort.'"[14]

A spiritual battle waged on three fronts

If you are committed to the Lord Jesus Christ, if you are growing spiritually, if you are dedicated to following the Lord's example and sharing his message with others, then chances are you are fiercely embroiled in a spiritual battle today. If you seek to do God's will, you will face opposition. You'll probably suffer wounds and losses in the course of your spiritual warfare. Don't be dismayed. Your commander has sent you a message. "Hold the fort; I am coming. Jesus."

In James 4, the apostle reminds us that a key sign that we are growing as Christians is that we find ourselves engaged in a battle of epic proportions. He writes:

What causes quarrels and what causes fights among you? Is it not this, that your passions are at war within you? You desire and do not have, so you murder. You covet and cannot obtain, so you fight and quarrel. You do not have, because you do not ask. You ask and do not receive, because you ask wrongly, to spend it on your passions. You adulterous people! Do you not know that friendship with the world is enmity with God? Therefore whoever wishes to be a friend of the world makes himself an enemy of God. Or do you suppose it is to no purpose that the Scripture says, "He yearns jealously over the spirit that he has made to dwell in us"? But he gives more grace. Therefore it says, "God opposes the proud, but gives grace to the humble." Submit yourselves therefore to God. Resist the devil, and he will flee from you. Draw near to God, and he will draw near to you. Cleanse your hands, you sinners, and purify your hearts, you double-minded. Be wretched and mourn and weep. Let your laughter be turned to mourning and your joy to gloom. Humble yourselves before the Lord, and he will exalt you (4:1-10).

James describes a war that is waged on three fronts: the flesh, the world, and the devil. The Christian life is warfare, a battle we must fight on all three fronts as we make our journey home. Satan is doing everything in his power to prevent us from growing spiritually. He uses the enticements of this sinful world. He appeals to the weakness of our fallen flesh. And he attacks us directly, assaulting our thoughts and emotions. The flesh, the world, and the devil have combined forces in a three-pronged attack aimed at keeping you in your spiritual infancy.

The first enemy: the flesh

James writes of the first of these enemies, the flesh, in the first three verses of chapter 4: "What causes quarrels and what causes fights among you? Is it not this, that your passions are at war within you? You desire and do not have, so you murder. You covet and cannot obtain, so you fight and quarrel. You do not have, because you do not ask. You ask and do not receive, because you ask wrongly, to spend it on your passions." When James speaks of our "passions," he speaks of our weak and fallen flesh—what is sometimes called "the old nature" or "the sin nature."

In our fleshly desires and ambitions, we fight and quarrel with each other. We struggle with our family members and our brothers and sisters in the church. We selfishly envy each other, we complain and fight, and our motives are tainted with self-centered desires. We are born with the inclination to sin, and this fleshly inclination remains with us even after we have committed our lives to Christ and are born again. This is the legacy we have inherited from our first parents, Adam and Eve.

When you confess Jesus Christ as your Lord and Savior, the old nature—the old self that filled you with envy, bitterness, jealousy, selfishness, lust, and pride—becomes like a deposed dictator. You can choose to yield to that deposed dictator and put him back in power—or you can choose to live in the liberty and peace of the new nature God has created in you through the power of the Holy Spirit.

Let me give you an example of this principle from history. Idi Amin was the military dictator of Uganda from 1971 to 1979. During his reign of terror, he murdered more than 350,000 Christians in order to force the Islamic religion on that country. When he was deposed, he fled to the arms of his Muslim brothers in Saudi Arabia.

For decades, until his death in 2003, Amin was alive in exile. He had no power in his home country of Uganda. He could do nothing to harm the free citizens of Uganda—yet thousands of Ugandans remained loyal to him and wanted to put him back in power. Of their own free will, they chose to place themselves under the spell of this powerless dictator. Their continued allegiance to Idi Amin put them in continual conflict with the democratic government of free Uganda.

Many Christians are like those Ugandans who remained loyal to their brutal dictator. God has deposed the dictator of the old nature, the flesh. That dictator no longer has the right to dominate our thoughts, our habits, our speech, our behavior, and our lives. Yet we choose to give power to this deposed dictator. As a result, our old nature continues to be in conflict with the new nature that Christ has given us.

Before we came to Christ, we would rationalize our sin. We would give our aching conscience a shot of Novocain to anesthetize ourselves against the pain of guilt and shame. But now, Christ has come into our lives. He has given us a new nature, a spiritual nature. This new nature is completely incompatible with the old sin nature of the flesh. In order to live victoriously in Christ, the new nature must win that battle by the power of God's Holy Spirit.

Murdering and coveting

Every time you let the old nature, along with its selfishness and self-centeredness, regain control, you end up in conflict and turmoil with people around you. Our selfish desires produce destructive actions. As James says, "You desire and do not have, so you murder. You covet and cannot obtain, so you fight and quarrel."

You may say, "I may have fought and quarreled now and then, but I have never murdered anyone! What is James talking about?" Have you ever spread any juicy gossip about someone? Have you ever criticized people behind their backs? Have you ever told stories about anyone that would put that person in a bad light? There's a term for that kind of behavior. It's called "character assassination." You don't kill people *physically*—you merely kill their reputations, break up their friendships and relationships, and leave them suffering and wounded. You may never have murdered anyone, but have you ever assassinated someone's character?

When James speaks of murder, he undoubtedly recalls the words of Jesus in the Sermon on the Mount:

> "You have heard that it was said to those of old, 'You shall not murder; and whoever murders will be liable to judgment.' But I say to you that everyone who is angry with his brother will be liable to judgment; whoever insults his brother will be liable to the council; and whoever says, 'You fool!' will be liable to the hell of fire. So if you are offering your gift at the altar and there remember that your brother has something against you, leave your gift there before the altar and go. First be reconciled to your brother, and then come and offer your gift" (Matthew 5:21-24).

Have you ever been angry with your Christian brother or sister and said things that should never be said? Have you ever insulted someone in the heat of the moment? Have you ever called someone an insulting name, such as, "You fool!"? This, the Lord says, comes from the same place in the human flesh that murder comes from. No follower of Christ should ever unleash such words and actions, because they come from the flesh, the old sin nature.

Selfish desires are dangerous. The flesh, our legacy from the Fall, is deceitful and destructive. If we don't defeat the flesh and replace it with Christlikeness, it will destroy us.

James writes, "You covet and cannot obtain, so you fight and quarrel" (4:2). These words remind us of the Tenth Commandment: "You shall not covet your neighbor's house; you shall not covet your neighbor's wife, or his male servant, or his female servant, or his ox, or his donkey, or anything that is your neighbor's" (Exodus 20:17). When covetousness takes over your life, it can lead you to break any or all of the other nine commandments.

When you covet someone's possessions or position or authority, bitterness and vindictiveness become a way of life. If there is a war going on inside you, sooner or later there is going to be a war on the outside. People at war with themselves because of selfish, covetous desires are always unhappy people. They are never thankful for the blessings they receive from God because they are too busy complaining about the blessings they don't have.

Covetous desires lead you not only into the wrong actions but also into praying the wrong prayers. James writes, "You ask and do not receive, because you ask wrongly, to spend it on your passions" (4:3). Instead of seeking the will of God for your life and counting it all joy, you tell God what he is supposed to do for you. And if God doesn't obey you, then you become angry with him and resentful toward him.

Your anger and resentment toward God eventually spills over into your relationships with his people. You become angry with those whose prayers are being answered. You covet what they have and believe that God has mistreated you and let you down. Why doesn't God give you the things you pray for? It's because you are praying with the wrong motive. You are asking wrongly, to spend his blessings on your fleshly passions rather than on service to God and others.

The second enemy: the world

Next, James writes about another enemy we face in our spiritual battles: the world. He writes: "You adulterous people! Do you not know that friendship with the world is enmity with God? Therefore whoever wishes to be a friend of the world makes himself an enemy of God. Or do you suppose it is to no purpose that the Scripture says, 'He yearns jealously over the spirit that he has made to dwell in us'? But he gives more grace. Therefore it says, 'God opposes the proud, but gives grace to the humble'" (4:4-6).

The phrase "the world" appears many times throughout Scripture. When God speaks about "the world," he does not mean the great outdoors or the natural beauty of Planet Earth. He is usually talking about the fallen world system that is controlled by Satan. The root cause of every war (whether internal human conflict or external conflicts between nations) is rebellion against God—and the world system is in a state of continual rebellion against God. The fallen world system began with Adam and Eve in the Garden of Eden, and that rebellious, fallen world system continues to defy God to this day.

Many Christians, unfortunately, are caught up in the fallen world system. They are friends of the world, and by their friendship, they have made themselves enemies of God. You might ask, "But how can a believer declare war against God?" James said we do this by loving the world, by befriending God's enemies, by fraternizing with the very systems of this world that deny God and his power and his Word.

We can fall into a state of friendship with the world very gradually, without even realizing it has happened until it's too late. At the beginning, we say, "I will go into that worldly situation to be a witness and a testimony for Christ." Then we begin to rationalize: "I need to get a little more involved in worldly things so that unsaved people can relate to me." Eventually, we don't even bother to rationalize or make excuses. We have compromised our values and our faith. We have become a friend of the world and an enemy of God. We have become part of the fallen world system.

James even describes friendship with the world as a form of adultery. "You adulterous people!" he writes. "Do you not know that friendship with the world is enmity with God?" (4:4). He uses the metaphor of adultery because believers, as part of the bride of Christ (the church), are married to Christ. So we ought to be faithful to Christ alone. Going out and becoming friends with this fallen world is analogous to a bride going out and being unfaithful to her husband.

The Jewish Christians who first received the letter from James understood exactly what the apostle meant when he said "You adulterous people!" The prophets Ezekiel, Jeremiah, and Hosea had used the very same figure of speech to rebuke the Hebrew people for their sin of compromise.

The apostle Paul wrote about a man named Demas, a former companion who had accompanied Paul on his missionary journeys: "For Demas, in love with this present world, has deserted me and gone to Thessalonica" (2 Timothy 4:10a). Demas had succumbed to the lure of the world and had deserted Paul.

We have to wonder how many Demas-like Christians are in the church today. Their lives do not give glory to God. They are in love with this present world, and they live as enemies of God. And we also have to wonder: Have they deserted the faith because they never knew Christ to begin with? Are they saved by faith—but only by the skin of their teeth? God alone knows the true state of every person's heart. But why would any believer want to take the chance of missing out on eternity for the sake of living as a friend of the world?

When this world becomes all you see and know and care about, you will befriend it, you will love it, you'll become one with the world—and you will be, as James so pointedly puts it, an adulterous person, an enemy of God.

In the 1700s, in the parish of Hackney in the city of London, there lived an Englishman named John Ward. Little is known about him today except that he was very rich and he served as a member of Parliament, in the House of Commons, until he was convicted of forgery and imprisoned in 1727. Ward is remembered today by the nickname "The Hackney Miser" because of a document found in his papers after his death—a document that has come to be known as "The Miser's Prayer." It reads:

> O Lord, Thou knowest that I have nine estates in the City of London, and likewise that I have lately purchased one estate in fee simple in the County of Essex; I beseech Thee to preserve the two counties of Middlesex and Essex from fire and earthquakes; and as I have a mortgage in Hertfordshire, I beg of Thee likewise to have an eye of compassion on that county; and for the rest of the counties thou mayest deal with them as Thou art pleased. O Lord, enable the Bank to answer their bills, and make all my debtors good men. Give a prosperous voyage and return to the "Mermaid" sloop, because I have insured it; and as Thou hast said the days of the wicked are but short, I trust in Thee that Thou wilt not forget Thy promise, as I have purchased an estate in reversion, which will be mine on the death of that profligate young man, Sir J.L. Keep my friends from sinking, and preserve me from thieves and housebreakers, and make all my servants so honest and faithful that they may attend to my interests, and never cheat me out of my property, night or day.[15]

Here was a man who was a friend of the world. He expected God to bless his worldly greed and selfishness. He prayed that God would bless the counties where he had investments, but gave God permission to do with all the other counties as he pleased. He prayed that God would keep all his servants and debtors honest. And he also made a speculative investment in an estate of a certain "Sir J.L.," trusting that God would cause this young man to die at a young age so that Mr. Ward could reap a handsome profit.

Those who make friends with the world and its corrupt system of values are always out for themselves. People who are out for themselves always pray the wrong prayers—and, like John Ward, they frequently end up in disgrace.

The third enemy: the devil

James goes on to write, "But he gives more grace. Therefore it says, 'God opposes the proud, but gives grace to the humble.' Submit yourselves therefore to God. Resist the devil, and he will flee from you" (4:6-7).

It's important to notice that we fight our spiritual battles on three fronts, and each front corresponds to one of the three Persons of the Trinity. The world is in conflict with God the Father. The flesh is at war with the Holy Spirit. And the devil opposes the Son of God.

What is the great sin by which Satan fell? Pride. And pride is therefore one of Satan's chief weapons in his battle against the saints and their Savior. God's goal for our lives is to make us Christlike and humble. Satan's goal for our lives is to erase Christ's image within us by making us selfishly proud.

What was Satan's promise to Eve in the Garden of Eden? He said, "When you eat of [the forbidden fruit] your eyes will be opened, and you will be like God." Eve believed him, and she ate of the fruit.

God wants us to depend on his grace. Satan wants us to depend on ourselves. Satan wins the victory over us when he inflates our egos and entices us into going our own way. We see this principle vividly illustrated in the hours before Jesus went to the cross. Jesus warned Simon Peter, "Simon, Simon, behold, Satan demanded to have you, that he might sift you like wheat, but I have prayed for you that your faith may not fail. And when you have turned again, strengthen your brothers."

But Peter wouldn't listen. He was full of prideful self-assurance. "Lord," he said, "I am ready to go with you both to prison and to death."

Jesus, who knew Peter more completely than Peter knew himself, replied, "I tell you, Peter, the rooster will not crow this day, until you deny three times that you know me." (See Luke 21:31-34.)

Later, the soldiers and religious leaders came to arrest Jesus in the Garden of Gethsemane. Peter—who was still being sifted like wheat by Satan—again acted out of pride and the desire to do things his way. He drew his sword and struck the high priest's servant, cutting off the man's right ear. One again, Jesus rebuked Peter, saying, "Put your sword into its sheath; shall I not drink the cup that the Father has given me?" (See John 18:10-11.)

Peter wanted to accomplish God's will in his own prideful way. James warns us against falling prey to Satan's enticement to pride. The devil doesn't mind in the least if you and I try to accomplish God's work—*so long as we try to do it in our own prideful way*. His goal is to keep us from obeying the will of God.

So these are the three enemies that continually conspire against us and seek to turn us away from God—the world, the flesh, and the devil. Paul tells us that these three enemies are the remnants of our old life of sin:

> And you were dead in the trespasses and sins in which you once walked, following the course of this world, following the prince of the power of the air, the spirit that is now at work in the sons of disobedience—among whom we all once lived in the passions of our flesh, carrying out the desires of the body and the mind, and were by nature children of wrath, like the rest of mankind (Ephesians 2:1-3).

Like James, Paul lists all three of our spiritual enemies: "the course of this world," "the passions of our flesh," and the devil, "the prince of the power of the air, the spirit that is now at work in the sons of disobedience." Christ has delivered us from these enemies. They cannot claim us and defeat us—but they still attack us.

Three keys to victory

How can we overcome these three enemies? How can we be friends of God and enemies of the world, the flesh, and the devil? James gives us three keys to enjoy peace instead of war.

The First Key: Submit to God

James writes, "Submit yourselves therefore to God. Resist the devil, and he will flee from you" (4:7). Submission is not a popular concept in our society. We live in an age that prizes rebellion and defiance over submission. The Greek word that is translated "submit" is borrowed from the military culture. It's a term that means, "Get into your proper rank."

An army operates on a hierarchy of authority, and those of lesser authority must submit to those of greater authority. If a private or a corporal takes it upon himself to begin acting like a general, trouble follows. Unquestioning obedience and unconditional submission are essential to military victory.

We see this same principle in the home. Children need to submit to parents. God places parents in authority over children for their own good and for the good of the family. Children must obey and be under the authority of the parents. The child may not agree with the parents and may not like what the parents decree. But children are blessed by God when they submit to parents and honor parents. This is especially true in times when the reasons for the parents' decisions may not be clear.

We also see this principle at work in the church. God has ordained leadership in the church. Because church leaders are human beings, they will never be perfect. You may not agree with the leaders of the church, but God has placed those leaders in a position of authority. You, as a believer and a church member, must "get into your proper rank" and submit to the authority of the church.

Submission to rightful leadership is always a key to victory and blessing. If you are in a church where you believe that the leaders are actually sinning and disobeying God, then perhaps you should find a church that has godly leadership, as you define it. But don't expect to be able to hop from church to church until you find one where the leaders agree with you 100 percent of the time.

We may not like what the government does, we may not agree with the decisions of our local and national leaders, but God has ordained government so that people may live in a peaceful, orderly society. Because government is ordained by God, we are to submit to its laws. Unless the government issues a decree that directly conflicts with the laws of God, we are to submit to the government. We are to "get into our proper rank" as citizens.

This same principle works in the spiritual realm. As Christians, we are all at war, facing enemies on three fronts. But James has given us the strategy for victory. If you want to win the battle over the flesh, the old nature, then submit all areas of your life to God. And if you want to win the battle over the devil, if you want to resist Satan and send him fleeing in panic, then submit all areas of your life to God. And if you want to overcome your enemy, the world, then submit all areas of your life to your almighty Friend, your Father in heaven.

The strategy is submission. And those who do not obey the strategy or those who refuse to submit and get into their proper rank as followers of Christ will pay a high price for their insubordination.

We see this principle at work in the life of King David. After he committed adultery with Bathsheba, he was at war with God. For a while, King David tried to keep a lid of silence on his scandal of adultery and murder. In Psalm 32, David recalled:

> For when I kept silent, my bones wasted away
>   through my groaning all day long.
> For day and night your hand was heavy upon me;
>   my strength was dried up as by the heat of summer.
> (Psalm 32:3-4)

That's what it feels like to be at war with God. David discovered that there is a high price to pay for enmity with God. But after the prophet Nathan confronted David with his sin, and David confessed and repented, his friendship with God was restored. In Psalm 51, he wrote:

> Purge me with hyssop, and I shall be clean;
> wash me, and I shall be whiter than snow.
> Let me hear joy and gladness;
> let the bones that you have broken rejoice.
> Hide your face from my sins,
> and blot out all my iniquities.
> Create in me a clean heart, O God,
> and renew a right spirit within me.
> Cast me not away from your presence,
> and take not your Holy Spirit from me.
> Restore to me the joy of your salvation,
> and uphold me with a willing spirit.
> (Psalm 51:7-12)

Those who are truly friends with God experience the peace of God's presence and the joy of their salvation.

The Second Key: Draw near to God

James writes, "Draw near to God, and he will draw near to you. Cleanse your hands, you sinners, and purify your hearts, you double-minded" (4:8). How do we draw near to God?

First, we draw near to God by confessing our sins to him and asking for his cleansing. What is the one thing that hinders us from drawing near to God? Sin. When there is sin in our lives, we don't want to listen to the prompting and conviction of the Holy Spirit. So we choose to draw away from God. We clutch our sins and push God away.

What does it mean, then, to draw near to God? It doesn't merely mean going to church or a Bible study. We can engage in religious activities, including church attendance and Bible study, while remaining far from God. Countless Christians sit in the pew Sunday after Sunday but never draw near to God.

Drawing near to God is not an activity. It is intimacy. It is the act of meeting God intimately, talking to him, listening for the voice of his Spirit within us, listening to his voice speaking to us through the Scriptures. It is the act of being honest with ourselves and with God about our sins, our failures, and our ungodly habits. It is the act of coming clean and repenting, of asking his Spirit to fill us, of renewing a right relationship with God.

When you experience that kind of intimacy with God, you will know that you have been with him and you have heard him speak to your heart. And you'll know that he has heard you and embraced you. Cleanse your hands. Purify your heart. Draw near to God, and he will draw near to you.

The Third Key: Humble yourself before the Lord

James writes, "Be wretched and mourn and weep. Let your laughter be turned to mourning and your joy to gloom. Humble yourselves before the Lord, and he will exalt you" (4:9-10).

Did you know that it is possible to outwardly submit to God without inwardly submitting? What does it mean to inwardly submit to God? It means humbling ourselves before God. It means that we realize the wretchedness of our sin. We mourn and weep over the sins we have committed. We lament and grieve and feel sorrow over our sins. We become sensitive to the awful burden of our sin. We recognize how our acts and habits of sin grieve the heart of our heavenly Father. That is what it means to humble ourselves before the Lord.

Tears signify brokenness. Tears are the mark of repentance. Tears are the evidence of submission.

It used to bother me when I would become tearful in public. When I preached in church, the very thought of my own wretchedness compared with the glory of Christ would bring me to tears—and it depressed me that I could not control my emotions in front of an audience. In my private prayer times, I often wept before God over my sin and unworthiness, and I felt that was the appropriate place for tears, not in public.

But after a while, I sensed that the Lord was rebuking me and telling me that I should not be ashamed of my tears. When my tearful emotions came forth, God used my tears to teach others about what a believer's brokenness is like. He used my public brokenness to reach the hearts of people in the congregation. Jesus said, "Blessed are those who mourn, for they shall be comforted" (Matthew 5:4). And the psalmist said,

> The sacrifices of God are a broken spirit;
> a broken and contrite heart, O God,
> you will not despise.
> (Psalm 51:17)

There is nothing that God despises more than pride and arrogance, whether it is the arrogance of position, status, wealth, power, family, fame, or religion. God loves humility and a broken spirit. But pride and arrogance is that sin by which Satan fell, and by which Satan still tries to ensnare us all.

A final word of caution

James closes this section with a final word of caution regarding a critical and judgmental spirit:

> Do not speak evil against one another, brothers. The one who speaks against a brother or judges his brother, speaks evil against the law and judges the law. But if you judge the law, you are not a doer of the law but a judge. There is only one lawgiver and judge, he who is able to save and to destroy. But who are you to judge your neighbor? (4:11-12).

If there is one thing that will stunt your growth as a Christian, it is a critical spirit. So James tells us we must stop speaking evil of one another, stop judging one another, stop criticizing one another. All of these sins come from one source: the satanic sin of pride.

After all, when we criticize someone else, what are we doing? We are exalting ourselves! We put others down to lift ourselves up. We make others look bad to make ourselves look better. When we judge another person, we are saying, in effect, that we have the right to judge them because we are morally superior to them.

A critical person is always a prideful person. You never see a critical, judgmental person who is genuinely humble. When we judge others and speak evil against them, we are saying that God is not the judge—we are. We are putting ourselves in God's place, on his judgment throne.

You may wonder, "What does this final warning from James have to do with the 'big three,' the world, the flesh, and the devil?" I assure you, it has everything to do with it. When we criticize each other, especially in the church, we invite our enemy into the heart of the church itself. It's as if we have opened the gates of our fortress and invited our enemy to walk right in and take over. When we attack each other in the church, we let loose the world, the flesh, and the devil in our midst to wage war against our brothers and sisters in Christ, and yes, against ourselves.

When we criticize and judge one another, we forget who our real enemy is. We are so busy treating each other as the enemy that we forget we are at war with the world, the flesh, and the devil. Your brother in Christ is not your enemy. Your sister in Christ is not your enemy.

Do not hand Satan a victory on a silver platter. Be aware of his bag of tricks and don't fall for them. Resist Satan and send him fleeing. Draw near to God, submit yourself to him, and humble yourself before him—and you will send Satan away in defeat. Be at peace with your brothers and sisters in the Lord; accept and forgive them—and seek their forgiveness as well.

If you do these things, you will deny Satan any victory over you or the church. Remember that the devil is a defeated enemy thanks to the empty tomb of Jesus. The risen Lord Jesus is with us, and he makes his power available to us if we will ask him.

Earlier in this chapter I told the story of the Battle of Allatoona Pass during the American Civil War. An eyewitness of those events, Major Daniel Webster Whittle, recalled how the message from General Sherman, "Hold the fort; I am coming," became the rallying cry and the turning point of that battle.

In civilian life, Daniel Whittle worked closely with evangelist Dwight L. Moody and Moody's musical director, the noted hymn writer Philip Bliss. Whittle's account of that battle inspired Bliss to compose a hymn titled "Hold the Fort." As you fight the good fight of faith against the world, the flesh, and the devil, remember the words of this hymn—and remember that Jesus, your Commander, is coming:

> Ho, my comrades! see the signal waving in the sky!
> Reinforcements now appearing, victory is nigh.
>
> *Refrain:*
> "Hold the fort, for I am coming," Jesus signals still;
> Wave the answer back to Heaven, "By Thy grace we will."
>
> See the mighty host advancing, Satan leading on;
> Mighty ones around us falling, courage almost gone!
>
> See the glorious banner waving! Hear the trumpet blow!
> In our Leader's Name we triumph over every foe.
>
> Fierce and long the battle rages, but our help is near;
> Onward comes our great Commander, cheer, my comrades,
> cheer! [16]

9

God's Plan and Our Plans

During World War II, General Douglas MacArthur needed to get his forces across a river. He consulted with his chief engineer and asked, "How long would it take to build a bridge across that river?"

"Three days," the engineer replied.

"Go ahead and draw up the plans."

Three days later, MacArthur was growing impatient to see the plans, so he summoned the engineer and asked, "Where are the plans for that bridge?"

The engineer seemed surprised by the question. "General," he said, "the bridge is ready. You can cross it now. But if you want the plans, you'll have to wait a little longer. We haven't finished those yet."[17]

As Christians, we are a lot like General MacArthur. We get focused on our plans. Meanwhile, God is at work building bridges, preparing for the advance of his kingdom. In the concluding section of James 4, the apostle warns us against focusing on our plans and forgetting the work that God is doing:

> Come now, you who say, "Today or tomorrow we will go into such and such a town and spend a year there and trade and make a profit"—yet you do not know what tomorrow will bring. What is your life? For you are a mist that appears for a little time and then vanishes. Instead you ought to say, "If the Lord wills, we will live and do this or that." As it is, you boast in your arrogance. All such boasting is evil. So whoever knows the right thing to do and fails to do it, for him it is sin (4:13-17).

These verses build on the previous theme of submission. As we saw in the first section of James 4, we are engaged in a war on three fronts, and our three enemies are the world, the flesh, and the devil. The first key to defeating our enemies and growing spiritually is the key of submission. James wrote, "Submit yourselves therefore to God." James reminds us that even as we make our plans, we must submit ourselves and our plans to the will of the Lord.

Unfortunately, all too many Christians view God's will for their lives as a kind of bitter medicine to be taken like castor oil. This, of course, is another one of Satan's lies. Satan wants us to distrust God and to be skeptical of his plans for our lives. So we need to be reminded that God's will for us is truly the evidence of his vast love for us.

Nothing to fear from God's will

When I gave my life to Jesus Christ in 1964, I was immediately on fire for the Lord. I would witness to anyone, anyplace, anytime. Though I was eager to share the gospel with others, I didn't want a career as a pastor. So when I became aware that God was calling me into the ministry, I rebelled. Like the prophet Jonah, I decided to run from God. I tossed my faith overboard and for eighteen months I wandered away from the Lord. I lived a lie. I went to church but my heart was cold. What made things worse, my mother died, and the devil began to sell me another lie: "If God really loved you, he would not have taken your mother away when you needed her the most." Why did I wander from the Lord? The answer is simple: I didn't want to submit myself to the will of God. I wanted to make my own plans for my life, and I didn't want *God's* plans to derail *my* plans. So, in my incredible foolishness, I thought I could escape from him. But our sovereign God, in his loving mercy, did not permit me to wander for more than eighteen months.

I look back at my younger self, and I'm amazed that I actually feared God's will for my life. Yet, I have met many people over the years who have the same fear. They are afraid to submit to God, afraid to abandon themselves to Christ. As I talk to them, I usually find that they fear God's will because they think they will have to swallow bitter medicine.

So James tells us that we must not leave God's good and perfect will out of our calculations. When we make our plans, we need to remember that God's plans are eternal and unchangeable, whereas our plans are contingent, fleeting, and subject to change. We don't know what tomorrow will bring, but we do know that all of our tomorrows are in God's hands. The purpose of this life is for us to learn to trust him more and more and to build our lives on *his* plan, not our own.

A few years ago, a young woman confessed to me she was afraid to commit her life to Christ. I asked her why. She said, "I'm afraid that if I receive him as Lord of my life, he will send me to some Third World country—and I don't want to go!"

I knew she was an animal lover, so I said, "If it were raining and storming outside, and you saw a cat outside your window, what would you do?"

At that point, she began to cry. "Say no more," she said.

For the first time, she was able to see her life from God's perspective. God doesn't want to make us miserable. He doesn't want to ruin our lives. He wants the best for us. He wants to save us from the drenching, freezing storms of life and bring us into his cozy, warm house. We have nothing to fear from our loving heavenly father. The will of God comes from the heart of God. His will is an expression of his love. When we submit to the will of God, we open our lives to the love of God. When we resist his will, we resist his love.

To be mature is to be dependent

In our culture, we identify *dependence* with *immaturity*. No creature is more helpless and dependent than a newborn baby. The baby becomes a toddler and learns to walk. The toddler becomes a child and learns to feed himself. The child becomes an adolescent, then a teenager, then a young adult, and at each stage of development, he becomes increasingly more independent.

But when a person comes to Christ, this picture is inverted. Baby Christians, new and immature in the faith, have a natural tendency to resist God's will. The more mature they become as Christians, the more dependent they are on God's will and the more willing they are to submit to his will. The most mature Christians of all are those who are the most dependent on God. They have given up all resistance to his will and have learned that God's love is always good, pleasant, and dependable.

Christian maturity means that we depend on God more, not less. Our dependence on God begins with our admission that we are helpless to save ourselves, and we must turn to Jesus for salvation. Some people think that the old saying "God helps those who help themselves" is a Bible verse—but that idea does not come from Scripture. It is 100 percent unbiblical. God helps those who quit trying to help themselves and lean completely on him.

When good King Asa of Judah faced the vastly superior army of the Ethiopians and all seemed hopeless, he cried out, "O LORD, there is none like you to help, between the mighty and the weak.

Help us, O Lord our God, for we rely on you" (2 Chronicles 14:11a). Asa relied on God, not his own strategy or the might of his nation, and the Lord delivered the land of Judah from the enemy.

Again and again, the psalmist David cried out to God in utter helplessness and dependence, and God helped him:

> Some trust in chariots and some in horses,
>   but we trust in the name of the Lord our God.
> (Psalm 20:7)

> O Lord my God, I cried to you for help,
>   and you have healed me.
> (Psalm 30:2)

> Behold, God is my helper;
>   the Lord is the upholder of my life.
> (Psalm 54:4)

> Help me, O Lord my God!
> Save me according to your steadfast love!
> (Psalm 109:26)

God is looking for men and women who have stopped trying to help themselves and seek God's help, God's power, and God's will instead. God seeks to raise up an entire generation of people who are not independent of him, not standing on their own two feet, but who are utterly, helplessly dependent on him. He wants mature Christians who daily experience the fulfillment of living under his complete control.

That goes against our grain, doesn't it? In our culture, men resist the idea of submission because they feel that submission—even submission to Almighty God!—somehow compromises their manhood. And women, who embrace the idea that they are liberated and empowered, also hate the idea of submission as a challenge to their feminism and femininity.

We have to get past this false notion that submission to God somehow robs us of our rights and our rightful identity. This false idea is actually robbing us of the essence of our Christian experience and Christian maturity. If you have never truly submitted to God, then you have never experienced the amazing power that comes with complete dependence on him.

The message of James in this passage is, "Stop overplanning your life. Don't forget that God has a plan for you. Submit yourself to God's plan and live in complete dependence on him—then watch what happens!"

Our lives are a mist, a vapor, here today and gone tomorrow. Our plans for the future are undependable and subject to change. If we want our lives to count, if we want our efforts to have lasting meaning and eternal purpose, then we must submit ourselves to his plan. We must join ourselves to his purpose.

I'm not saying there is anything wrong with planning for the future. I believe in setting goals. I'm sure that James does not condemn either plan-making or goal-setting. He does not suggest that we should simply drift through life aimlessly, without any plan for the future. Rather, James is saying, "Don't make plans based on selfish desires and ambitions, and then say, 'Lord, bless my plans.'" The Word of God and the will of God must be at the very heart of all our plans and goals.

Sleeping in the back of the boat

Whenever I sit down to make plans or set goals, I take a day out to fast and pray. I ask the Lord, "What do you want me to accomplish in the coming year? How many people do you want me to lead to you this coming year? How much should the church budget be for the coming year? What areas in my life do you want me to change?"

I go through the list of unmet needs, unsolved problems, and other challenges in my life and ministry, and I lay them out before the Lord and ask for his guidance and direction. As the Lord gives me impressions of what he wants me to do, I begin to pray for what God wants in my life. I don't want these goals to be *my* goals, *my* selfish ambitions. I truly want to follow God's plan. I want my prayer life to be centered around his leading for my life.

The psalmist wrote, "Delight yourself in the LORD, and he will give you the desires of your heart" (Psalm 37:4). We like to focus on the desires of our hearts. But we need to remember that delighting ourselves in the Lord means that we seek only his will for our lives. When we delight in the Lord, he not only fulfills our desires, but he gives us the right desires, the godly desire to do his will and live in dependence on him. Jesus put it this way:

> "Abide in me, and I in you. As the branch cannot bear fruit by itself, unless it abides in the vine, neither can you, unless you abide in me. I am the vine; you are the branches. Whoever abides in me and I in him, he it is that bears much fruit, for apart from me you can do nothing. If anyone does not abide in me he is thrown away like a branch and withers; and the branches are gathered, thrown into the fire, and burned. If you abide in me, and my words abide in you, ask whatever you wish, and it will be done for you" (John 15:4-7).

If you abide in the Lord's Word, if you seek only his will for your life, then you will ask only for what is his will. Whatever you ask will be done, because everything you ask will be in alignment with God's will for your life.

Does God reveal everything to us? No. Much about God's will is mysterious and unknown to us. He is a sovereign God.

But as long as I know that God is in control, I am at peace. Even when I make mistakes, even when I mishear God, misread his will, or misinterpret his voice, I know he is in control. After falling flat on my face, I can come back to God and say, "Lord, teach me the lesson of this mistake I've made. Tell me where I got ahead of you. Tell me how I have misinterpreted or disobeyed your voice."

Until you recognize that God is in control and you willingly submit to his lordship, you will cause yourself all kinds of grief and stress. When you surrender, when you cease resisting and submit to his loving plan for your life, you will experience peace and joy.

In Luke 8, we encounter the story of Jesus sleeping in the back of the boat during the storm on the Sea of Galilee. In this account we see two distinct reactions to the storm. First, we see the disciples' reaction—a reaction of panic and terror in the face of the storm. Second, we see the Lord's reaction—he slept peacefully in the back of the boat.

Why did the disciples panic? They had forgotten that the Lord himself was in control. If you are facing stress, fear, or anxiety right now, then you can identify with the disciples. You are in panic mode because you have forgotten that the Lord is in control.

You can deal with your stress right now by making a choice— a decision to live a life of dependence on God. Christians who live with stress and anxiety do so because they are determined to take control of their lives. But Christians who live in dependence on God experience peace and serenity. They can sleep in the back of the boat even though the boat is being tossed by the storm.

The measuring stick of maturity

You may wonder, "How can I know if I'm growing spiritually or not?" You might be surprised to know there is a measuring stick you can use to see if you are experiencing spiritual growth. Here it is: Measure the amount of time between the moment you began to fret or stress or worry about a certain problem and the moment you relinquished that situation to the Holy Spirit. In other words, how long does it take for you to let go and let God take over?

The shorter that period of time, the more you are trusting God and the more you are growing spiritually. The shorter that period of time, the sooner you are tuning in to the voice of God. The goal of the Christian life is to continually increase your trust in God and your submission to God, while decreasing the amount of time it takes to turn it all over to him.

As we have previously seen, we are engaged in a three-front war against the world, the flesh, and the devil. These three enemies are working continuously to keep us from listening to the voice of God. The great tragedy of the church is that so many Christians are unable to hear God's voice.

Many Christians live their lives as if they are in a room full of talking people, with the stereo and television at full blast, while trying to carry on a telephone conversation with God: "What's that, Lord?...I can't hear you!...Could you talk a little louder?...Oh, what's the use!" They can't hear the voice of God at all, so they go through their lives, lurching from crisis to crisis, constantly stressed, never trusting.

I once heard a story about a man who sat in a waiting room, eager for his chance to interview for a job as a wireless operator. This was back in the days when a great deal of communication was transmitted by Morse code, and a stream of dots and dashes could be heard over a loudspeaker in the room. A number of other applicants were in the room, and they were all talking among themselves.

But this one man was not talking. He was listening.

Suddenly, he jumped up, rushed into the employer's office, and was gone for several minutes. When he returned, he announced, "The rest of you can go now. I got the job!"

The other applicants were incensed. "How did you get in ahead of us?" they asked.

"If you hadn't been so busy talking, you might have noticed there was a message in Morse code playing on a loudspeaker. It said, 'I need a man who is always alert. The first man to hear this message and come into my office gets the job.'"

And so it is with you and me. We cannot hear the voice of God if we don't listen for it. If we do not hear his voice, then we cannot be in tune with his will. And if we are not in tune with his will, the plans we make for our life will not be God's plan—and we will miss God's best for us.

If you are not in tune with God, chances are that your life is not going well, and you are sick and tired of it. When we try to live apart from the will of God, we inevitably suffer for it. When God cannot rule, he overrules. When Jonah would not let God rule, God overruled in his life. When I would not let God rule, God overruled in my life.

You may ask, "How can I know the will of God?" We find the answer in John 7, in which a number of religious leaders hear Jesus teaching in the temple at Jerusalem and they marvel at his words, because he teaches with authority though he has never studied in a rabbinical school. Jesus answered them, "My teaching is not mine, but his who sent me. If anyone's will is to do God's will, he will know whether the teaching is from God" (7:16-17). In other words, if you are willing to obey God and do his will, God will reveal his truth and his will to you.

God does not reveal his will to those who are merely curious, or those who want to impress others with their Bible knowledge. God reveals his will to those who want to obey him. If you want to know God's will, but you have no intention of obeying his will, God will not reveal it to you. As Paul writes, God wants us to be "filled with the knowledge of his will in all spiritual wisdom and understanding" (Colossians 1:9). And God tells us that he wants us to "understand what the will of the Lord is" (Ephesians 5:17).

Where does spiritual maturity come from? It doesn't come from cramming our heads with knowledge. It doesn't come from the mere passage of time. It comes from submission to God. It comes from obedience to God. It comes from trust in God.

And remember, you don't need to fully understand God's will in order to do his will. Even a five-year-old child understands this concept. Sometimes a father says, "Do this now," and the child asks, "Why?" Often, the father's only answer is, "Because I said so." The father has a good reason for his command, but the child lacks the maturity to understand that reason. When the child is older and more mature, he will probably understand, but for now, the child must simply trust and obey.

We don't always understand why God does what he does, allows what he allows, and commands what he commands. We are God's spiritual five-year-olds. But the more we trust, the more mature we will become. And with increasing trust and obedience comes greater understanding.

In time, through trusting and obeying God, we become God's friends. He gives us the privilege of knowing him, a better understanding why he does what he does. Jesus put it this way: "No longer do I call you servants, for the servant does not know what his master is doing; but I have called you friends, for all that I have heard from my Father I have made known to you" (John 15:15).

The apostle Paul reminds us, "Do not be conformed to this world, but be transformed by the renewal of your mind, that by testing you may discern what is the will of God, what is good and acceptable and perfect" (Romans 12:2). What does he mean, "by testing you may discern" God's will? "Testing" means proving God's will by putting it into practice. We *test* his will and *prove* his will by *doing* his will. When we obey God's will and apply it in our lives, we prove that his will is good, acceptable, and perfect. And the more we obey, the easier it becomes to know and do what God wants us to do.

Learning to do the will of God is like learning to swim or learning to play a musical instrument. The more you practice it, the more you master it—and the more it becomes second nature to you. Usually, those who repeatedly ask, "How do I discern God's will for my life? How can I learn what he wants me to do?," are announcing to the world that they have never really tried to do God's will.

The sand in our spiritual shoes

Many of us, in our slow journey toward spiritual maturity, move from resistance to God's will to a place of grudging, reluctant obedience. We see this in the life of Jonah. He knew that God wanted him to go and preach to Nineveh, but he resisted God's will, ran away, and ended up in the belly of a big fish. The fish deposited Jonah on the shore, so Jonah picked himself up, walked to Nineveh, and did what God told him to do in the first place.

But Jonah's obedience was a grudging and reluctant obedience. He didn't preach to Nineveh with all his heart. He didn't preach out of a love for God and he certainly had no love for the people of Nineveh. He did what God commanded him to do simply to avoid further disciplinary action.

Is your obedience to God like Jonah's? If so, then you may be accomplishing God's work but missing all the blessings God has for you. Instead of experiencing the joy of serving God, you are merely toiling to get it over with. God wants you to obey with joy and enthusiasm.

Why should we joyfully obey God's will? James explains that we should do so because life is so uncertain. It is foolish to lay out our plans for tomorrow without taking account of God's plan for us. You and I may not be around tomorrow. Life is like a mist. It appears for a while, and then it vanishes. We all pass away. Only the things we have done in obedience to the will of God will last.

Young people tend to think they are invincible. They don't have a sense of the fragility and brevity of life. In their early twenties, young people usually begin to develop a sense that life has an endpoint—and we never know where that endpoint might be. Occasionally, a young person loses a friend to a car crash or a drug overdose, and he or she is confronted with the harsh fact of human mortality. The realization hits: "Oh no! Someday, I'm really going to die!"

But time passes. People get involved in life and eventually fall back into thinking it will go on forever. So James concludes by saying, "So whoever knows the right thing to do and fails to do it, for him it is sin" (4:17). In other words, if we know God's will for our lives, but we continue on, making our self-centered plans while ignoring God's call, we are committing sin.

Throughout the New Testament, sins of omission are treated just as severely as sins of commission. Knowing the right thing to do and not doing it is sin, just as surely as it is sin to willfully break God's commandments.

Jesus made his point vividly and powerfully in Matthew 25, where he said that at the final judgment, all the people would be gathered before him, and he would separate the people as a shepherd would separate sheep from the goats. And to the one group he would say,

> "Come, you who are blessed by my Father, inherit the kingdom prepared for you from the foundation of the world. For I was hungry and you gave me food, I was thirsty and you gave me drink, I was a stranger and you welcomed me, I was naked and you clothed me, I was sick and you visited me, I was in prison and you came to me" (Matthew 25:34-36).

And then he would explain that when these people did these good deeds for needy people, they did it for the Lord himself.

Then Jesus said he would turn to the other group and say, "Depart from me, you cursed, into the eternal fire prepared for the devil and his angels" (25:41). And these other people would be shocked and bewildered and protest that they had done nothing wrong. And the Lord's reply would be that they saw people who were hungry, thirsty, needy, and destitute—and they did nothing! They had no compassion. They showed no love. Theirs was not the sin of commission but of omission. And so they were sent away into eternal punishment.

Sin is not just the wrongs we commit. Sin is also the right actions, the compassionate actions, that we fail to commit.

Someone has said it's not the mountain you climb that wears you out, it's the grain of sand in your shoe. Many of us worry about the mountain we are climbing when we should pay more attention to the grain of sand in our shoes. Many of us need to stop before we take another step—and check our shoes. It may be that the reason we are struggling and failing in the Christian life is not because of some great sin we are committing but because we have been:

- indifferent toward what is right
- indifferent toward our Christian convictions
- indifferent toward the work of the kingdom of God
- indifferent toward what God hates
- indifferent toward what God wants us to do
- indifferent toward the truth that is being trampled on

What is your attitude toward the will of God? Do you make your own plans and decisions in complete disregard of God's will for your life? Do you know God's will for your life—but you refuse to obey it? Are you obeying God's will—but grudgingly and reluctantly? If you answer yes to any of these questions, then I encourage you to check your shoes for that grain of sand that is wearing you down.

I'm not saying that your life will be easy if you do the will of God. I'm very sure it won't be. But I can absolutely guarantee that if you know God's will, love God's will, and cheerfully do God's will, you will enjoy his blessings. Your life will be richer, more joyful, and filled with the peace that passes understanding.

After Jesus ministered to the woman at the well in Samaria, his disciples came to him and brought him food to eat. But Jesus said, "I have food to eat that you do not know about…My food is to do the will of him who sent me and to accomplish his work" (John 4:32-34).

May his food be your food and mine as well.

10

Managing God's Money

Randy C. Alcorn, in his book *Money, Possessions, and Eternity*, recounts the woes of the rich. "I have made many millions," said John D. Rockefeller, founder of Standard Oil Company, "but they have brought me no happiness." Railroad magnate William Henry Vanderbilt was the richest man in the world at the time of his death. Near the end of his life, he said, "The care of $200 million is enough to kill anyone. There is no pleasure in it." John Jacob Astor (1763–1848) was the first multimillionaire in America, having made his fortune in real estate, fur trading, and opium smuggling. He once said, "I am the most miserable man on earth." Pioneer carmaker Henry Ford once said, "I was happier when doing a mechanic's job."[18]

If you thought the apostle James was a blunt, pull-no-punches straight talker in the first four chapters of this letter, wait until you hear him talk about money! He opens chapter 5 with some straight talk about riches, a section that could well serve as a commentary on the laments of Rockefeller, Vanderbilt, and other millionaires:

Come now, you rich, weep and howl for the miseries
that are coming upon you. Your riches have rotted and
your garments are moth-eaten. Your gold and silver have
corroded, and their corrosion will be evidence against
you and will eat your flesh like fire. You have laid up treasure in the last days. Behold, the wages of the laborers
who mowed your fields, which you kept back by fraud,
are crying out against you, and the cries of the harvesters
have reached the ears of the Lord of hosts. You have lived
on the earth in luxury and in self-indulgence. You have
fattened your hearts in a day of slaughter. You have condemned and murdered the righteous person. He does
not resist you (5:1-6).

Money is a sensitive topic. The subject of rich and poor in our
society and in the church is enough to ignite a third world war.
There were many wealthy people in the church at the time James
wrote this letter, and the apostle was clearly not trying to ingrati-
ate himself when he proclaimed God's Word to them. In this passage, James deals with our attitude toward money as much as our
use of money.

Most of us have strong opinions about money. Those who are
just scraping by on a modest income tend to resent the rich. And the
rich tend to be defensive about their riches. Nowhere in the Bible
does it say that it is a sin, in and of itself, to be wealthy. Numerous
Bible heroes were people of great wealth. One was the patriarch
Abraham, a man of immense wealth who, the Bible tells us, walked
with God. And God used this wealthy, godly man to bless the
whole world. Other Bible heroes of substantial net worth include
Job, David, Solomon, Jehoshaphat, Hezekiah, the women who sup-
ported the ministry of the Lord Jesus, the Roman centurion who
believed in Jesus, Joseph of Arimathea (who provided the burial
tomb of Jesus), Philemon, Barnabas, and Lydia.

So it's clear that the message of the apostle James is not aimed at rich people as an economic class. He's not saying it's a sin to be wealthy. Rather, James is addressing those who use their wealth in a way that is sinful and destructive to others. Undoubtedly, many people in the first-century church didn't like hearing a sermon about money, just as many people don't like hearing such sermons today. Unfortunately, many people have made a god out of their wealth. They are sensitive about the subject of money because they have made money their god, and they don't want anyone to attack their god.

There are two ways to respond to James's sermon. We can either surrender our money to God, or we can surrender to the Money God. If you are *not* rich, you may be thinking of tuning out this chapter, thinking, *James is just talking to the rich. Nothing in this passage is relevant to me.* Please keep reading, because I believe there is something in this passage for everyone, whether rich or poor or in between.

Who is rich, who is poor?

According to the U.S. Census Bureau, more than thirty million Americans, roughly one-seventh of all Americans, live in "poverty." But what is poverty in America? While it is true that there are people in America who are homeless or hungry and not able to meet their basic needs, the average person defined as poor by the government has a higher standard of living than most people would imagine.

James Quinn Wilson, a political scientist who teaches at Pepperdine University and Boston College, has looked at the census data and concludes, "The poorest Americans today live a better life than all but the richest persons a hundred years ago." The data show that the typical poor household in America has a car, air conditioning, two color televisions, cable or satellite TV service, a DVD player, a refrigerator, oven and stove, a microwave, a clothes washer and dryer, a cordless phone, and a coffeemaker. If there are children in the home, the typical poor family has a game system such as an Xbox or PlayStation.[19]

Now, compare this level of poverty with the destitution that is commonplace in other parts of the world. The World Bank defines "absolute poverty" as a state of being deprived of such basic human needs as food, clean drinking water, clothing, shelter, sanitation, health care, and education. The World Bank estimates that 1.29 billion people live in these conditions around the globe.[20]

So even those our government defines as poor live like kings and queens compared to a huge segment of the world's population. This is not to make light of the plight of the needy in America. But it's important for us to gain a realistic perspective on what constitutes real poverty and real wealth. The richest person in the first-century church was an absolute pauper compared with any average middle-class American. So if you think the message of James 5 does not apply to you and me—*think again*!

People used to view the human race as being divided into two classes, the "haves" and the "have-nots." Today, however, we recognize a third class of people: the "have-not-paid-for-what-they-haves." It seems that when people finally realized that money cannot buy happiness, they tried to buy happiness with credit cards.

James said,

> Come now, you rich, weep and howl for the miseries that are coming upon you. Your riches have rotted and your garments are moth-eaten. Your gold and silver have corroded, and their corrosion will be evidence against you and will eat your flesh like fire. You have laid up treasure in the last days (5:1-3).

The apostle is writing to those who have made money their god, who place their trust in wealth, and who use their wealth selfishly. It's no sin to be rich, but it's a serious sin to be self-centered, miserly, lacking in compassion, and indifferent to the needs of your fellow human beings. Wealth is a blessing, and those who are blessed with wealth should not squander it on selfish wants or use it to lord it over others. Those who are blessed with wealth should use it to bless others.

If the making of money and the hoarding of money are your consuming passions, James warns that one day you will wake up on the other side of life—and you will have nothing. You will not even have the Lord's righteousness to carry you safely into eternity because you placed your trust in riches, not in God. That is why James says to the greedy rich, "Weep and howl for the miseries that are coming upon you" (5:1). You will be weeping and wailing throughout eternity, so you might as well start now.

That's why the apostle Paul urges his colleague in ministry, Timothy, to instruct those who are rich in this present world not to be conceited or to trust in uncertain riches: "As for the rich in this present age, charge them not to be haughty, nor to set their hopes on the uncertainty of riches, but on God, who richly provides us with everything to enjoy" (1 Timothy 6:17).

Almighty dollar or Almighty God?

James has previously said that life is uncertain: "[Y]ou do not know what tomorrow will bring. What is your life? For you are a mist that appears for a little time and then vanishes" (4:14). Now he reminds us that money too is uncertain and must be surrendered and submitted to God.

Most people think, *If only I had a million dollars, or ten million dollars, or fifty million dollars, I'd be set for life. I wouldn't have a care in the world.* That's why so many people buy lottery tickets—they hope that Fortune will tap them on the shoulder and magically transform them into millionaires and they'll live happily ever after. But that rarely happens.

A Michigan woman who won a $1 million lottery prize in 2011

was disgraced a few months later when the state discovered that she was collecting food stamps and other welfare benefits in spite of her lottery winnings. About a year after winning the lottery, this young mother of two was found dead of a suspected drug overdose.[21]

A Texas man won $31 million in the state lottery, so he bought a ranch, homes for himself and family members, cars for his wife and kids, and even made a huge contribution to his church. But soon it seemed that more and more friends, fellow church members, and even strangers were pestering him for loans and donations. He fought continually with his wife over his inability to say no to people. Finally, less than two years after his big win, this "lucky" lottery winner committed suicide.[22]

An Englishman nicknamed "the Lotto Lout" won £9.7 million in the United Kingdom's lottery, and within eight years he had spent it all on drugs, gambling, and prostitutes; today he lives on welfare. A New Jersey woman hit that state's lottery twice, once in 1985 and again in 1986, collecting a total of $5.4 million; within a few years, she had gambled it all away and was living in a trailer. In 1998, a Pennsylvania man won $16.2 million in that state's lottery. Soon afterward, his brother hired a hit man to try to kill him in a failed scheme to steal his money, and other people talked him into a series of bad investments that left him bankrupt. He died penniless at age sixty-six in 2006.[23]

Riches tend to give us a false feeling of self-sufficiency. I once read of an immigrant who said that he came to America with a loaf of bread in one hand and sixteen cents in the other—and he parlayed that tiny pittance into a financial empire and a lavish lifestyle. He concluded, "Look at what I have been able to do without God."

You might think you would never fall into that same trap, but there's something about acquiring riches and possessions that tricks us into thinking we did it all ourselves. Instead of seeing the wealth we have acquired as a blessing from God, we easily begin thinking,

Look at all that I have accomplished! Look at what I achieved through my brilliance and hard work!

It is so easy for us to allow the almighty dollar to occupy the place in our lives that belongs to Almighty God. When money provides for all our needs, makes us comfortable, keeps us entertained, enables us to feel complete and in control, and fills us with the pride of success, it's easy to think, *What do I need God for? I did this all myself!*

That is the error of self-satisfied pride talking, and the moment we start to think this way, we are out of the will of God. God himself should complete us and control our lives. He alone is supposed to meet all our needs and be our comfort. His work should be our diversion. Knowing that God is the author of our success should keep us humble and make us grateful.

Whom do you trust?

Why does James tell us it is pointless and futile to amass wealth for our own selfish use? I think the apostle may have been thinking of the words of Jesus in the Sermon on the Mount: "Do not lay up for yourselves treasures on earth, where moth and rust destroy and where thieves break in and steal, but lay up for yourselves treasures in heaven, where neither moth nor rust destroys and where thieves do not break in and steal" (Matthew 6:19-20).

What happens to all the wealth you have accumulated when your mortal life comes to an end? Estate taxes will take a large portion, and your heirs will probably squander whatever remains. As someone has said, a miser isn't much fun to live with, but he makes a wonderful ancestor. As Solomon once observed:

> I hated all my toil in which I toil under the sun, seeing
> that I must leave it to the man who will come after me,
> and who knows whether he will be wise or a fool? Yet
> he will be master of all for which I toiled and used my

wisdom under the sun. This also is vanity (Ecclesiastes 2:18-19).

The Egyptian pharaohs thought they could take it with them, so they had all their treasures buried along with them to ensure their comfort and financial security in the afterlife. But all they did was make a few grave robbers very rich.

Many Christians, if they are honest, must confess that they place much more trust in their investments—their 401(k)s, their mutual funds and money market funds, the gold in their hidden wall safe—than they do in God. And it's prudent, of course, to invest and save for the future—there's no sin in that. But what is the source of our security? Is it our treasure in heaven? Or is it the treasure we have stored up on earth?

James tells us, "Your gold and silver have corroded, and their corrosion will be evidence against you and will eat your flesh like fire. You have laid up treasure in the last days" (5:3). We hear a lot today about gold and silver as sound investments, but James says the corruption of our gold and silver will eat our flesh like fire. Strong language!

History shows that even gold is undependable as an investment. The price of gold averaged $615 per ounce during the economic crisis of 1980, but had lost about half its value when recovery was in full swing in 1985. By 2001, gold was worth only $271 per ounce. The economic crisis of 2008 sent the price of gold soaring again, and as I write these words during the still-troubled economy of 2013, an ounce of gold sells for more than $1700. Today's gold sellers tell you that if you invest in gold now, you will see the price rise to $2000 or $3000 an ounce. But what if it plunges back to 2001 levels? No one knows. All we know is that there is no genuine security in gold or silver at any price.

Some people like to cherry-pick Scripture verses to make the claim that God is opposed to wealth. But an objective study of Scripture shows that wealth is a blessing from God. In the Old

Testament, God established Israel and set forth specific rules for gaining and securing wealth—and he warned Israel to trust in the Giver of the wealth, not in the wealth itself. God said, "Beware lest you say in your heart, 'My power and the might of my hand have gotten me this wealth.' You shall remember the LORD your God, for it is he who gives you power to get wealth, that he may confirm his covenant that he swore to your fathers, as it is this day" (Deuteronomy 8:17-18).

God is the great real-estate magnate of the Old Testament. He settled the Hebrew people in the Promised Land and gave them the choicest real estate so they could be blessed and could benefit from the wealth of the land. God is the great entrepreneur and CEO of the Old Testament. He established Israel as the economic powerhouse of the region, especially under King Solomon's reign. In those days, wealth poured into Israel from all over the known world, including such distant lands as India, the Arabian Peninsula (where the Queen of Sheba ruled), and parts of Africa.

Leftists and liberation theologians would have us believe that Jesus was a proto-Marxist who rejected capitalism and private ownership of property. But read his parable of the workers in the vineyard in Matthew 20:1-16 and you will see that Jesus clearly respects private property, free enterprise, and voluntary trade. Nowhere does God's Word condemn private ownership or the making of money or the profit motive. What is consistently condemned throughout Scripture is greed, selfishness, acquiring wealth through dishonesty or theft, the unfair exploitation of workers, the use of wealth to control and oppress others, a lack of compassion toward those who are genuinely in need, and an attitude of entitlement (those who say, "The world owes me a living").

The message of James 5 is that those who acquire wealth by exploiting and cheating other people are under the judgment of God. If God invests his blessings in your life, he expects you to use those blessings to reap dividends in the lives of others. If you squander his blessings entirely on yourself and your selfish ambitions, you place yourself in great danger.

Is James warning of the danger of hell? I don't believe he's saying that. If a rich man has genuinely trusted Jesus Christ as Savior, his salvation is assured by the atonement of Jesus Christ. At the same time, a person who claims to believe in Christ, yet whose life does not demonstrate the compassion of Christ, the values of Christ, and the obedience of Christ, should ask himself, "Do I genuinely belong to Christ or not? Where is the evidence that he is my Savior if I do not obey him as Lord?"

It doesn't matter to God whether you are rich or poor. Wealth and poverty are simply circumstances of life. What matters to God is whether you trust in him, whether your heart is obedient to him, and whether the faith you profess is genuine. Whom do you trust for your security? Do you trust in wealth? Do you trust in yourself? Or do you trust in the Lord Jesus Christ?

If you cannot say with absolute certainty that you have surrendered your life to Jesus as Lord and Savior, I urge you to do so today, right now, before you turn this page.

God always knows

Believers who abuse the blessing of wealth risk the consequences of their sin. Paul tells us that our deeds as Christians will be evaluated: "For we must all appear before the judgment seat of Christ, so that each one may receive what is due for what he has done in the body, whether good or evil" (2 Corinthians 5:10).

The judgment Paul speaks of is not the judgment of hell and condemnation. It is the judgment that determines whether you will receive an eternal reward for your service to the Lord—or whether you will barely escape into heaven by the skin of your teeth. The way you have used your money as a believer will be tested by fire. As Paul wrote in his first letter to the Corinthians:

Now if anyone builds on the foundation with gold, silver, precious stones, wood, hay, straw—each one's work will become manifest, for the Day will disclose it, because it will be revealed by fire, and the fire will test what sort of work each one has done. If the work that anyone has built on the foundation survives, he will receive a reward. If anyone's work is burned up, he will suffer loss, though he himself will be saved, but only as through fire (1 Corinthians 3:12-15).

If we mishandle our blessings and prove ourselves to be selfish stewards, our work will be incinerated at the judgment seat. The believer's use of money is so important that Jesus devoted sixteen of his thirty-eight parables to the godly management of money and possessions. One-tenth of the verses in the four gospels deal directly and pointedly with the subject of money. The Bible contains about five hundred verses on prayer, five hundred verses on faith—*and more than two thousand verses* on money and possessions.

Why does God's Word place such great emphasis on our finances? God knew that money would always be a powerful force in our lives and would always have an enormous hold over us. He knew we would naturally tend to put money on the throne of our lives, where he rightfully belongs. He knew that we would mistakenly look to money for our security, our sense of well-being, and our sense of worth and purpose. He knew we would be inclined to work and sacrifice for money and center our lives around money, instead of focusing our lives on him.

Many of us tend to confuse money with life. This confusion was illustrated by the famed comedian of the forties and fifties, Jack Benny, who liked to portray himself as the stingiest man in the world. In one of his famous comedy sketches, he is walking along the street when he is accosted by a masked gunman who demands, "Your money or your life!" Benny's only response is a long-drawn-out silence. The gunman growls, "I said, your money or your life!" Benny snaps, "Don't rush me! I'm thinking it over!"

It seems ridiculous that a man would risk his life over the cash in his wallet. Yet many of us have made such a god of money that we are willing to risk our eternal reward and even our eternal destiny for the sake of our possessions. Even though God has clearly warned us in his Word that he is watching how we use our money and possessions, we often behave sinfully and selfishly with our money, and we close our hearts to the suffering around us. God has set an example for us, blessing us with wealth. Do we follow his example? Do we bless others?

Life says to us, "Your money or your eternal reward!" And for some reason, that's a difficult choice for us, and we respond, "Don't rush me! I'm thinking it over!"

The way we use our wealth is important to God. We are fooling ourselves if we think we can conceal our actions from his eyes. If we sin with our wallets, our checkbooks, our credit cards, and our debit cards, God knows. If we sin by acts of commission or acts of omission, God knows. If we close our hearts to the least, the last, and the lost, God knows.

As the writer to the Hebrews reminds us, "And no creature is hidden from his sight, but all are naked and exposed to the eyes of him to whom we must give account" (Hebrews 4:13). So when James warns the wealthy who have acquired their riches by cheating their workers of a fair wage, the wealthy need to know that the cries of the poor reach the ears of God in heaven. He knows, and nothing escapes his attention.

God knew that Adam and Eve ate the fruit (Genesis 3). God knew that Cain slew Abel (Genesis 4). God knew that Achan kept back the spoils from the conquest of Jericho (Joshua 7). God knew that David sinned with Bathsheba (2 Samuel 11). God knew that Jezebel had Naboth the Jezreelite murdered (1 Kings 21). God knew that Gehazi, the greedy assistant of the prophet Elisha, took the gifts

from Naaman the Syrian leper (2 Kings 5). God knew that Ananias and Sapphira lied about the price of the field they sold (Acts 5).
Don't kid yourself. You can't get away with robbing God. You
can't get away with greed and selfishness. You can't get away with
treating people unjustly. God always knows.

"I could have done more!"

Next, the apostle James underscores four perils of self-centered
prosperity. These are four roadblocks to our spiritual growth, four
reasons why some Christians never reach maturity in their walk
with God. James writes:

> You have lived on the earth in luxury and in self-
> indulgence. You have fattened your hearts in a day of
> slaughter. You have condemned and murdered the righ-
> teous person. He does not resist you (5:5-6).

First Peril: A life of luxury

Luxurious living is living to pamper ourselves with material
things, services, and a lifestyle designed to show off our affluence.
Luxury goods are nonessential goods that appeal to snobbery. His-
torically, a lifestyle of luxurious consumption was limited to the elite
classes and was designed to underscore the differences between the
classes. Now, of course, our culture is so awash in wealth that many
middle-class people live a lifestyle of conspicuous consumption—
and they simply charge their expensive entertainment, travel, and
purchases with credit cards. The "lifestyle of the rich and famous"
may inflate our egos, but it does nothing to honor God.

Second Peril: A life of self-indulgence

God has blessed us with many good things, and there is nothing
wrong with enjoying the blessings he showers on us. We go wrong
in our thinking when we begin to feel entitled to lavish our blessings on ourselves for our own personal comfort. We go wrong in our

thinking when we forget that God has blessed us so that we can do his work on earth and bless others.

As believers, we need to always remember that we come into this world with nothing and we leave it with nothing. In between, we are merely stewards of God's resources. As the true owner of these resources, he is going to come to us one day and ask for an accounting of how we managed his money. Will we be proud of our expensive restaurant tab? Our lavish vacations? The electronic entertainment gadgets we have accumulated? The mountain of debt we have piled up? If you "indulge till you bulge," you are hindering your spiritual growth and storing up judgment and regret for yourself in the Last Day.

Third Peril: A fattened heart in the day of slaughter

The image the apostle James suggests to us here is that of an animal, such as a calf or lamb, that has been fattened to be slaughtered. The animal knows only that its trough is filled with delicious food, so that animal gorges himself, fattens himself, enjoys himself—and never suspects that all of this luxurious food is intended only to prepare him for the slaughter.

Those who lavish God's material blessings on themselves so they can live a comfortable, luxurious lifestyle do not realize that the "day of slaughter," a day of accountability, is approaching. James is telling us that we reap what we sow. If we invest God's blessings in works of righteousness and compassion and charity toward others, we will reap the reward. But if we squander God's blessings on our selfish wants and pleasures, all of our "fatness" will turn into sorrow and regret in the day of slaughter.

Fourth Peril: Condemnation and murder of the righteous

James is speaking metaphorically here. He is not talking about rich people who literally kill their employees. He is saying that the love of money causes us to become coldhearted toward the needs of others.

So we trample others in order to acquire our wealth, sometimes by simply ignoring the needs of others and other times by actually attacking their reputations and destroying their careers. Businesspeople in the church sometimes compartmentalize their church lives and their business lives. They behave one way on Sunday at church, and they behave quite differently on work days at the office. They rationalize their hypocrisy by telling themselves that the business world is a dog-eat-dog world. They tell themselves that the only way to get ahead in business is to lie, cheat, exploit people, and destroy reputations. Sure, people get hurt—but that's just the way this game is played.

The problem is that God expects us to be his witnesses, his ministers, his ambassadors wherever we go, including the dog-eat-dog business world. If that means we miss out on a promotion or a major business deal, then so be it. If we have to play the game with one hand tied behind our backs in order to maintain our Christian testimonies, then so be it. If we are clawing our way up the business ladder, and trampling others on our way to the top, then God can't use us as a witness and a minister of his grace—and we can't spiritually grow.

Steven Spielberg's film *Schindler's List* tells the true story of Oskar Schindler, a factory owner in German-occupied Poland during the Holocaust. Though Schindler (portrayed by Liam Neeson) is a flawed man in many ways, he has a heart full of compassion toward the Jewish slave laborers in his factory. He risks his own life and safety to save Jews from death in the concentration camps.

Near the close of the film, Schindler is surrounded by scores and scores of Jewish people he has rescued. One of them, an old man, steps forward and presents a letter to Schindler. It is a letter of thanks, signed by all the people he has saved. Then the man gives Schindler a gift of a gold ring, inscribed with a line from the Talmud: "Whoever saves one life saves the world entire."

Oskar Schindler is deeply moved, and at first it seems that he is touched by their gratitude. But it soon becomes clear that Schindler is not touched by gratitude but by his own guilt and remorse. "I could have gotten more out," he says in a grief-stricken voice. "I could have gotten more—"

The old man says, "Mr. Schindler, there are eleven hundred people alive because of you!"

But Oskar Schindler is wracked with emotional pain. "I threw away so much money! You have no idea! I didn't do enough! Why did I keep my limousine? I could have sold it and bought ten more people. And this gold pin in my lapel! It would have bought two more people! I could have gotten more people, and I didn't! I didn't!"

Today we live lives of luxury and self-indulgence, fattening our hearts as the final day approaches. But someday, God will demand an accounting. Will we say, "I did all I could with everything you gave me"? Or will we say, "I could have done more, but I didn't"?

When we stand face-to-face before God, what will our answer be?

11

Jesus Is Right on Schedule

George Matheson was at the top of his class at the University of Glasgow, despite being almost completely blind. Soon after he graduated, his fiancée told him she was leaving him—she had decided she could not be the wife of a blind preacher. Though devastated by his fiancée's rejection, Matheson went on to seminary and was ordained to the ministry in 1868. The people of a small church in the seaside village of Innelan, Scotland, called him to be their pastor. He served in that congregation for years, and in time he thought he had put the pain of his fiancée's rejection behind him.

In 1882, his younger sister announced her impending marriage. Though Matheson was happy for his sister, he went into a deep depression. He was forty years old and alone. The festivities surrounding his sister's wedding reminded him of how abandoned he had felt when his own beloved announced she was leaving him. On the day of his sister's wedding, he later recalled, he experienced "the most severe mental suffering."

That night, unable to sleep, George Matheson felt God speaking to his soul, giving him the words of a song. Matheson took pen in hand and began to write. The song he wrote was a song about love—not romantic love, the kind of love that can change and fade away. He wrote about a love that never fails, a love that would never let go.

He later recalled, "I had the impression of having [the song] dictated to me by some inward voice rather than of working it out myself. I am quite sure that the whole work was completed in five minutes." These are a portion of the words God gave to George Matheson:

> O Love that wilt not let me go,
> I rest my weary soul in thee;
> I give thee back the life I owe,
> That in thine ocean depths its flow
> May richer, fuller be.

> O Joy that seekest me through pain,
> I cannot close my heart to thee;
> I trace the rainbow through the rain,
> And feel the promise is not vain
> That morn shall tearless be.

A man who had suffered heartbreak wrote about a love that never lets go. A man who was blind wrote of a rainbow glimpsed through the rain. Though George Matheson's sufferings had not changed, his perspective on his sufferings was transformed as God gave him a new song. It was a song of a man who had learned to be patient through trials.

Stand your ground!

As we come to the next section of the letter of James, we find that the apostle's advice to those going through trials and suffering is, "Be patient."

Be patient, therefore, brothers, until the coming of the Lord. See how the farmer waits for the precious fruit of the earth, being patient about it, until it receives the early and the late rains. You also, be patient. Establish your hearts, for the coming of the Lord is at hand. Do not grumble against one another, brothers, so that you may not be judged; behold, the Judge is standing at the door. As an example of suffering and patience, brothers, take the prophets who spoke in the name of the Lord. Behold, we consider those blessed who remained steadfast. You have heard of the steadfastness of Job, and you have seen the purpose of the Lord, how the Lord is compassionate and merciful (5:7-11).

Here, James has circled back to the opening theme of this letter: "Count it all joy, my brothers, when you meet trials of various kinds, for you know that the testing of your faith produces steadfastness. And let steadfastness have its full effect, that you may be perfect and complete, lacking in nothing" (1:2-4). James echoes his opening theme because he knows how much the early church was suffering, and how much Christlike patience the early believers needed in order to endure their trials. He wanted them to know that God would eventually heal all hurts and right all wrongs—but God would not fix everything until Jesus returned.

So the message of James in this passage is, "Look forward to that day! Let your expectation of the return of the Lord Jesus Christ be the source of your patience. Let the hope of that day be the source of the power you need to get through this day. Trace the coming rainbow through the present rain—and persevere!"

Three times in this passage, James reminds us of the approaching return of our Lord: "Be patient, therefore, brothers, until the coming of the Lord" (verse 7). "Establish your hearts, for the coming of the Lord is at hand" (verse 8). "Behold, the Judge is standing at the door" (verse 9). The apostle James echoes the words of Jesus before he went to the cross: "In the world you will have tribulation. But take heart; I have overcome the world" (John 16:33).

What does James mean when he tells us to be patient? The original Greek word James uses is actually stronger than our English word *patience*. In the Greek, the word actually means "standing your ground when you feel like running away." It's the kind of patience a soldier must demonstrate when he's caught in a cross fire and artillery shells are raining all around him. That soldier would like to be anyplace but where he is, but he stands his ground, he remains patient under fire, so that he can carry on the fight and win the victory.

What is the trial you are going through right now? You may be enduring a trial of suffering at your workplace. Your boss is harsh and overbearing, and your fellow employees are rude and insulting. Maybe they know that you're a Christian, and they are attacking you for your faith, your moral values, and your witness. Their attacks on you are relentless, and you know they will never let up. You'd like to just resign and get a new job, yet you feel that God has you there for a purpose. You have seen him open doors of ministry and use you to witness to others about Christ. Stay put until he tells you to stand down. When you hang in there, enduring the suffering with Christlike grace, you demonstrate patience under fire.

Or you may find yourself undergoing a trial in your marriage. You face daily conflict and tension. You feel attacked and misunderstood. Your spouse is unfair to you. You believe God is calling you to persevere and seek healing for the damaged relationship, but you are tired of the struggle. The temptation to bail out of the marriage grows stronger every day. Satan whispers, "You deserve better. Wouldn't you be happier in a relationship with this coworker or that neighbor?" Don't surrender to Satan's lies. Be patient and stand your ground. Continue to obey God and demonstrate patience under fire.

Or you may be a business owner, trying to be successful in a tough economy. You have pulled every lever, tried one marketing idea after another, worked eighteen-hour days, and still the money is not coming in. Your dream is dying. You are ready to walk away, to give up, and even to let go of your trust in God. But God is trying to teach you some important lessons through this experience. Don't surrender. Be patient and stand your ground. Go to God in prayer and ask, "Lord, what do you want me to learn through this time of testing and trial?"

When we go through times of suffering, especially when our sufferings are not of our own making, we have many questions: How can I be patient when everything is collapsing around me? How long must I wait? When is God going to answer my prayers for help?

James anticipates our questions and answers us with three encouraging examples of patient endurance. Through these examples, the apostle teaches us the secret of patiently standing our ground and waiting upon the Lord.

First example of godly patience: the farmer

The first example James gives us is that of a farmer. He writes, "See how the farmer waits for the precious fruit of the earth, being patient about it, until it receives the early and the late rains" (5:7). The farmer is patient. A farmer would be foolish to plant the seed on Monday, then go out Tuesday morning in hopes of picking fruit. He would be equally foolish to go out within a few weeks to dig up the seedlings to see how they are doing.

James wrote his letter to the Jewish culture of the first century. In Israel in that day, farmers would plow the fields and plant the seed during the fall months because the early rain would soften the soil for planting. Then the farmer would wait for the later rain in the spring, which would help to mature the harvest. So the farmer would have to wait patiently between the early rains of September and the late rains of April. But the farmer knows that the harvest will be worth the wait. It will be a day of joy and celebration when he gathers his crops.

The apostle Paul uses the same planting-and-reaping metaphor when he writes, "And let us not grow weary of doing good, for in due season we will reap, if we do not give up" (Galatians 6:9). In this analogy, our hearts are the soil, the seed is the Word of God, and the harvest is spiritual growth and maturity. As you live out this biblical principle of planting, patience, and harvest, you will find there are seasons in the spiritual life just as there are seasons of planting and harvest.

Sometimes our hearts become wintry, cold, and unresponsive. At such times, the Lord must plow the hard soil of our hearts before he can plant the seed of his Word. Then he sends the rain and sunshine of his goodness to water and warm our hearts so that the seed he planted may germinate and sprout. We must not be impatient for fruit to appear, because growth and ripening take time. The fruit will come in time if we remain patient, practicing the principles God put in place at creation.

You may say, "Well, that's a nice metaphor. But how does that help me as I'm going through one of the toughest times of my life?" I urge you to remember that God is producing a harvest in your life. You want your life to bear fruit—and especially the fruit of the Spirit: love, joy, peace, patience, kindness, goodness, faithfulness, gentleness, and self-control (see Galatians 5:22-23). And God wants you to be productive in his kingdom, bearing the fruit of good works, righteousness, and a vibrant testimony to the world around you. And one of the ways God is able to bring forth fruit in our lives is through times of trial.

Our natural tendency is to be impatient farmers who expect the fruit to appear instantly and who keep digging up the plants prematurely. When our patience fails and we rip out the seedlings before they have a chance to mature, we force God to do what he does not want to do. We force him to plant the seed again. We force God to keep going over the same ground in our lives because we don't learn the lessons of our trials.

If you wait patiently in times of suffering, praying to God and praising God as you await his deliverance, God will bless you with a bountiful harvest of spiritual growth and maturity. That harvest will take place in his time, not yours. But it will take place. As your trust in God grows, he will establish your heart and strengthen your faith.

One aspect of the farmer metaphor that we easily forget is that farmers are never idle. Farmers are patient, and they wait for the seasons to come, but they don't spend their waiting time in a hammock, sipping lemonade. Farmers work hard throughout the year. They work on the barn and the silo, making sure there is plenty of storage for the harvest when it comes in. They work in the fields, pulling up weeds and maintaining a healthy environment for the crop. They don't just wait, they invest a lot of sweat and sore muscles into their waiting time.

The apostle James does not suggest that we should simply go up on the mountain and wait for the Lord's return, doing nothing in the meantime. Like the farmer, we are constantly working, witnessing, praying, praising, trusting, and studying God's Word so that he can bring forth a harvest of growth and maturity in our lives.

Jesus told his disciples a parable about a master of a house who went away to attend a wedding, leaving his servants in charge. When he came home, he found that some servants were ready for his return and some were not. Jesus concluded, "You also must be ready, for the Son of Man is coming at an hour you do not expect...Blessed is that servant whom his master will find so doing when he comes" (Luke 12:40,43). In other words, if we would be ready for the return of the Lord, then we must stay busy, doing the work of the Lord until he comes.

I heard an old Scottish preacher tell the story of a sailing ship returning to Scotland after many days at sea. As the ship neared the shore, the sailors lined the deck, gazing toward the dock where their loved ones had gathered to greet them. The skipper peered through binoculars and identified some of the wives who waved from the dock. "I see Bill's wife, Mary," he said, "and I see Tom's wife, Jane, and David's wife, Ann."

There was only one sailor on the ship whose wife was not on the dock. This sailor became frantic with worry. Why wasn't his wife there to greet him? Was she sick? Had she died? Had she run off with another man?

When the lines were secured and the ship was made fast to the dock, the sailor leaped from the ship, ran down the dock, and hurried up the hill to his cottage. He flung open the door—and his wife ran to him, threw her arms around his neck, and said, "I've been waiting for you!"

"Yes," the sailor replied in a tone of gentle rebuke, "but the other men's wives were *watching* for them."

Are you merely waiting for the Lord, or are you watching for him? Those who watch for the Lord are motivated to work while they are waiting. They are eagerly waiting and watching for his return.

In verse 9, James reminds us how we should treat our Christian brothers and sisters while we wait for the Lord's return: "Do not grumble against one another, brothers, so that you may not be judged; behold, the Judge is standing at the door."

Returning to the analogy of the farmer, we need to remember that farmers rarely waste time fighting with other farmers. Most farmers are helpful to one another. They lend a hand to one another. They encourage one another. They support one another. Farmers rarely waste energy on disputes because they have too much work to do.

James tells us that we should not grumble against our fellow Christians. We shouldn't pick fights with them, criticize them, gossip about them, or treat them as enemies. If we do, God will know and we will be judged.

If you have been involved in the church for any length of time, you have probably seen instances of Christians dividing and battling over minor issues—and even over nonissues. Often, fights between Christians are out-and-out personality conflicts or turf battles between two strong-willed individuals who want to be the boss. As Bible teacher Warren Wiersbe has said, "Impatience with God often leads to impatience with God's people, and this is a sin we must avoid. If we start using the sickles on each other, we will miss the harvest!"[24]

True spiritual maturity is demonstrated by a willingness to submit our wants, desires, and egos to the lordship of Jesus Christ. As we grow in Christlike character, we will see that the unity of the Lord's church is far more important than most of the petty issues we fight over.

Second example of godly patience: the prophets of God

The second example of godly patience James offers is that of the Old Testament prophets. He writes: "As an example of suffering and patience, brothers, take the prophets who spoke in the name of the Lord" (5:10).

When you are fully committed to following the will of God, yet you are facing obstacles and opposition, it's important to remember that other godly men and women have also suffered while doing God's will. Suffering is often a direct result of doing God's will. As Paul told Timothy, "Indeed, all who desire to live a godly life in Christ Jesus will be persecuted" (2 Timothy 3:12).

People often assume that if a Christian suffers, it must be the result of hidden sin or unfaithfulness. Remember, that's what Job's so-called "comforters" told him after he had suffered the cataclysmic loss of his wealth, his health, and his children. Accusing an innocent, suffering Christian of unrepentant sin or secret unfaithfulness is judgmental and arrogant. That person is already suffering illness, pain, or loss, and anyone who would accuse a suffering person of sin is being cruel. God sees the thoughts and motives of the human heart; we do not—so we have no right to judge our brothers and sisters in Christ.

Sometimes, innocent Christians are needlessly hard on themselves, saying, "If I'm suffering, then I must have done something terrible! I must have sinned without realizing it, and now God is punishing me for it. If only I knew what sin I committed!"

If you have been a faithful husband or wife and your spouse has walked out on you; or if you have been faithful parents and your child rebels against you; or if you have been a loyal employee yet your boss mistreats you; or if you have just been diagnosed with a life-threatening illness, or you have suffered a loss or setback—please don't automatically assume that you are being punished for sin. It may well be that God is trying to get your attention, but if that's so, the Holy Spirit will convict you of sin in your life. God is not going to simply hurt you, then leave you bewildered and confused.

We all suffer—even people who are in the center of God's will. Faithfulness to God does not guarantee freedom from suffering. The obedience of Jesus led him to the cross. The obedience of Paul got him stoned, lashed, shipwrecked, and imprisoned. The obedience of the disciples led to their martyrdom. And, as James reminds us, the obedience of the Old Testament prophets caused them to be persecuted. As we remember these bold and obedient prophets, their example inspires our courage and stamina to go on and be strong.

The prophet Elijah told wicked King Ahab there would be a drought in the land for three and a half years. Though Elijah himself suffered from the drought, God took care of him.

The prophet Daniel made a decision in his heart to obey God rather than men. That decision landed him in a den of lions—but God watched over him.

The prophet Isaiah spoke fearlessly for God during the turbulent collapse of the northern kingdom of Israel. Though Isaiah influenced King Hezekiah for the better, rabbinic tradition tells us that

Isaiah suffered persecution and was executed—cut in half by a saw—
at the order of Hezekiah's wicked son, King Manasseh of Judah.
The prophet Jeremiah suffered deep agony of spirit as he spoke
God's warnings to the people of Judah. He described the persecution he suffered at the hands of the people he had counted as friends:

> I have become a laughingstock all the day;
> everyone mocks me.
> For whenever I speak, I cry out,
> I shout, "Violence and destruction!"
> For the word of the LORD has become for me
> a reproach and derision all day long...
> For I hear many whispering.
> Terror is on every side!
> "Denounce him! Let us denounce him!"
> say all my close friends,
> watching for my fall.
> "Perhaps he will be deceived;
> then we can overcome him
> and take our revenge on him."
> (Jeremiah 20:7b-8,10)

Why are God's most faithful servants so often subjected to the
harshest of trials? Their obedience through suffering is a mighty
witness for the power of God. Their patience and endurance are an
eloquent testimony for Christ. As Paul wrote, "For whatever was
written in former days was written for our instruction, that through
endurance and through the encouragement of the Scriptures we
might have hope" (Romans 15:4).

The better you understand God's Word, the greater your encouragement from God during the fiery trials of life. So, like the farmer,
keep working. Like the prophet, keep witnessing. No matter how
trying and troubling your circumstances might be, remember these
examples and endure your trials with patience.

Third example of godly patience: Job

The third example of patient endurance is Job. James writes: "Behold, we consider those blessed who remained steadfast. You have heard of the steadfastness of Job, and you have seen the purpose of the Lord, how the Lord is compassionate and merciful" (5:11). Preacher and author A.W. Tozer once wrote, "It is doubtful whether God can bless a man greatly until he has hurt him deeply." And English evangelist Charles Haddon Spurgeon observed, "Is it not a curious thing that whenever God means to make a man great, he always first breaks him in pieces?" This principle is vividly illustrated in the life of Job, and Job himself expressed this principle in Job 23:10—"But [God] knows the way that I take; when he has tried me, I shall come out as gold."

There are many reasons why believers sometimes need to be broken in order to be greatly used by God.

- Believers need to know what victory means. No one can truly savor victory who has not first tasted defeat, and there are no victories without battles.

- Believers often have to learn to empathize and identify with hurting, oppressed people—and the best way to learn empathy for suffering people is by undergoing a time of suffering ourselves.

- Believers often need to learn to pray, and sometimes the best school of prayer is a time of suffering, loss, or crisis in our lives. We learn the value of prayer when we are driven to our knees.

- Believers need to learn to praise God in all circumstances, including praising him in times of suffering. As David wrote after going through a time of being hunted by King Saul and forced to hide in a cave, "Bring me out of prison, that I may give thanks to your name!" (Psalm 142:7a).

The apostle Paul described an experience in which he was taken to "the third heaven" and experienced marvelous things. Paul used a literary device of writing about himself in the third person, but later discloses that the man he is writing of is himself:

> I know a man in Christ who fourteen years ago was caught up to the third heaven—whether in the body or out of the body I do not know, God knows. And I know that this man was caught up into paradise—whether in the body or out of the body I do not know, God knows— and he heard things that cannot be told, which man may not utter (2 Corinthians 12:2-4).

God had given Paul a tremendous privilege that few other believers have experienced—and as a direct result of that experience, God also permitted Paul to suffer what he called a "thorn in the flesh." He wrote, "So to keep me from becoming conceited because of the surpassing greatness of the revelations, a thorn was given me in the flesh, a messenger of Satan to harass me, to keep me from becoming conceited" (2 Corinthians 12:7).

For some believers, God must balance privileges with responsibilities, joys with sorrows, blessings with burdens. This balance of experiences prevents us from becoming conceited. For the sake of our spiritual maturity, God brings us through experiences that keep us humble. You undoubtedly know from your observation of other people's children that pampering, overprotecting, and overindulging produces a spoiled and immature child. Spoiled children grow up to be spoiled adults.

God's goal for our lives is spiritual maturity, so he lovingly refuses to spoil us or overindulge us. This sometimes makes God seem harsh to us, just as a loving human father who says no to his children often seems overly harsh to them. But love—authentic parental love—does not permit children to grow up spoiled and stunted in their character.

Returning to Job, James's third example of godly patience, let's review some key points about the book of Job and what we can learn from it. The book divides into three sections. Part 1 (Job 1–3) describes Job's distress. Part 2 (Job 4–37) describes Job's defense. Part 3 (Job 38–42) describes Job's deliverance. First, God humbled Job, and then he honored Job. Clearly, Job didn't understand all that was happening in the spiritual realm. He knew nothing of the spiritual battle between God and his rebellious angel, Satan.

Job's circumstances were against him; he lost everything, including his children and his health. Job's wife was against him; she told him to curse God and die. Job's sufferings were compounded when his friends accused him of sin and hypocrisy. It even seemed to Job that God was against him, because when Job cried out to God for answers, he heard no reply.

Yet Job patiently endured!

Satan was absolutely certain that Job would crumble under the pressure and abandon his faith altogether. But Job proved Satan wrong. Yes, Job questioned God's will, he was hurt and bewildered, yet through it all, Job was able to say, "Though he slay me, I will hope in him; yet I will argue my ways to his face" (Job 13:15).

That is an amazing statement. Job was so sure of God's perfect justice that he felt confident that he could argue his case before God, even if God took his life. Do you and I have that kind of faith—a faith that trusts God so much that we dare to lay our feelings honestly before him, and we trust him not only with our lives but with death itself?

If you are going through a painful trial right now, and you know that you are not outside of God's will, not rebelling against him but trusting in him, you may feel bewildered. You may be questioning God. Your friends may have turned against you or falsely accused you. Your family may mistreat or misunderstand you. All your circumstances are working against you.

God has an exalted purpose for your suffering. I'm not saying that God inflicted this suffering on you, but I do know that he allowed it, just as he allowed the sufferings of Job. And I know that God never wastes an experience of suffering. There is always some benefit to be gained from our trials.

After his sufferings, Job met God in a new and deeper way—and God will likewise reveal himself to you. Just as God showered a double blessing on Job after his sufferings, he is preparing a double blessing for you. You may think, *If God is so merciful, why did he permit Job to go through this? He could have prevented Job's sufferings but he didn't.*

God knew what was going to happen in Job's life. My finite mind can't comprehend what God was doing, but I know that God was glorified and Job was purified through Job's trials. I believe God is following this same process in the trials you are going through right now. And I believe you will be blessed and made more mature in Christ if you patiently endure this trial.

Let your "yes" be yes and your "no" be no

When you are in a fiery furnace, remember that God's loving hand is on the thermostat. Satan wants you to become impatient with God. He wants to rob you of God's blessing in your life. Moses became impatient with God, and as a result, he forfeited his joy of entering into the Promised Land. Abraham became impatient with God, and his impatience resulted in the birth of Ishmael, whose descendants are the enemies of Israel to this day. Peter became impatient, and in his haste he drew a sword and tried to kill the servant of the high priest.

When Satan attacks us, he usually tries to provoke our impatience and send us blundering ahead of the Lord. When we get ahead of God, we lose certain blessings, especially the blessings of spiritual maturity. God's assurance to us in times of suffering is, "My grace is sufficient for you, for my power is made perfect in weakness" (2 Corinthians 12:9). God will transform Satan's attacks into grace and strength for building you up and making you more Christlike and spiritually mature.

When Satan turns up the heat, run to God and let him refresh your spirit. When the plowing becomes difficult and the planting becomes a struggle, remember that a glorious day of harvest is coming. When you don't see fruit instantly appear, remember that God's timing is perfect.

In the final verse of this section, James offers a word of counsel that may seem oddly unrelated to the issue of patient endurance, but is actually extremely relevant:

> But above all, my brothers, do not swear, either by heaven or by earth or by any other oath, but let your "yes" be yes and your "no" be no, so that you may not fall under condemnation (5:12).

In this verse, James echoes the command of Jesus in the Sermon on the Mount:

> "Again you have heard that it was said to those of old, 'You shall not swear falsely, but shall perform to the Lord what you have sworn.' But I say to you, Do not take an oath at all, either by heaven, for it is the throne of God, or by the earth, for it is his footstool, or by Jerusalem, for it is the city of the great King. And do not take an oath by your head, for you cannot make one hair white or black. Let what you say be simply 'Yes' or 'No'; anything more than this comes from evil" (Matthew 5:33-37).

When people of character and integrity are confronted about a sin or a mistake, they admit it, ask forgiveness, and move on. When people of integrity are wrongly accused, they do not feel they have to defend themselves or take an oath. They simply say "Yes" or "No," then let God be their Defender and Vindicator.

Over the years, there have been times when I have been personally criticized or The Church of The Apostles has been attacked in the media. Someone once asked me how I respond to such attacks. I replied, "I don't." Many years ago, my mother used to tell me, "Let God be your defender. He will do a much better job than you could ever do." And I heed my mother's advice to this day.

If you place your trust in God, you will endure with patience. Your season of trial will plant seeds of growth and fruitfulness, and all you have lost, all you have suffered, will be restored to you in the day of harvest. Your blessings will be multiplied beyond your expectations.

Just wait and see!

12

Limitless Power

In September 1857, the United States was a deeply troubled nation, bitterly divided over slavery and shaken by a global financial meltdown, the Panic of 1857. Joblessness was rampant, and public drunkenness was an epidemic in cities across America.

In New York City, where tens of thousands of unemployed men stood idle in the streets, a businessman named Jeremiah Lanphier listened to the leading of God. Lanphier organized a prayer meeting to be held on September 23, 1857, in a room at the North Dutch Reformed Church on Fulton Street in lower Manhattan.

That first meeting got off to an inauspicious start. For the first half-hour, Lanphier was the one and only participant. Then a second person joined him. A few others straggled in a little later, and it became a real prayer meeting. As Zechariah 4:10 reminds us, "Do not despise these small beginnings, for the LORD rejoices to see the work begin" (NLT).

Lanphier set forth a few simple rules for the meeting: There would be no preaching and no theological arguments. Participants would be welcome from every evangelical faith tradition. Denominational differences could not be discussed. Meetings would start promptly at noon, end promptly at one, and would focus on prayer. Participation would be spontaneous, but prayers were limited to five minutes duration.

Though only a handful of people attended the first meeting, twenty attended the second meeting. The third meeting, forty participants. During the fourth week, the participants decided to hold a meeting every workday—and soon hundreds and even thousands of business people were meeting daily at noon for prayer. These meetings became known as the Fulton Street Prayer Meetings, even though they were soon being held at other locations throughout the city. Before long, the movement had spread to nearby cities, then coast to coast, and ultimately to England and other countries.

Many nonbelievers attended these meetings and were so powerfully impacted by God that they gave their lives to Christ. Upwards of a million decisions for Christ were recorded. The evangelical movement that began in those prayer meetings gave birth to a number of ministries, including the Bowery Mission, the McCauley Street Mission, the Student Volunteer Movement, and the Salvation Army.

Do we still believe in the power of prayer? Do we still believe that Christians can come together, even in a "small beginnings" way, to pray and see incredible changes take place? Or have we lost our confidence in the power of prayer?

In the closing lines of his mighty epistle, the apostle James reminds us of the importance and power of prayer.

James was widely known as a man of prayer. St. Jerome (c. 347–420), who translated the Bible into Latin (the Vulgate edition), also wrote a book called *Lives of Illustrious Men*. In that book, he quoted the second-century church historian Hegesippus: "After the apostles, James the brother of the Lord surnamed the Just was made head of the Church at Jerusalem…He alone had the privilege of entering the Holy of Holies, since indeed he did not use woolen vestments but linen and went alone into the temple and prayed in behalf of the people, insomuch that his knees were reputed to have acquired the hardness of camels' knees."[25]

What a wonderful reputation to have! And what a glorious nickname to be known by: Old Camel-Knees! Can you imagine being such a man or woman of prayer that everywhere you go, people would point and say, "There goes Camel-Knees!" He was so respected as the head of the church in Jerusalem that the Jewish religious authorities granted him the privilege of entering the Holy of Holies, where he would go to his knees and pray for the people.

Acts 12 tells the story of how Peter was arrested by King Herod and was scheduled for trial and probable execution. The church, meanwhile, prayed earnestly for his release. Herod kept Peter in prison, bound with chains between two soldiers so he could not escape. But in the middle of the night, an angel came to Peter and said, "Dress yourself and put on your sandals. Wrap your cloak around you and follow me" (v. 8). And the angel led Peter out of the prison.

After his release, Peter went to the house where the believers were praying. They were so shocked at Peter's release that they could not believe it was true. Peter told the believers how God sent an angel to deliver him, then he said to them, "Tell these things to James and to the brothers" (v. 17). Why did Peter specifically ask them to tell this news to James? *Peter knew that James was interceding for him in prayer.* Peter wanted James to know, as soon as possible, that his prayers had been answered.

In view of James's reputation for prayer, it's not surprising that he concludes his letter with a strong exhortation on prayer. James underscores for us four main points about prayer in the last eight verses in his letter:

1. Pray in both good times and hard times (5:13).

2. Offer intercessory prayer for others (5:14-15).

3. Prayer releases the power of God (5:16-18).

4. Pray that you and your fellow believers will remain faithful (5:19-20).

Let's look at each of these in turn.

Pray in both good times and hard times

In verse 13, James writes:

> Is anyone among you suffering? Let him pray. Is anyone cheerful? Let him sing praise (5:13).

Are you going through hard times? Are you suffering? Then it's time to pray. Are you going through good times? Is your heart full of gladness? Then it's time for a prayerful song of praise to God.

Unfortunately, many of us pray only when times are hard. We do not think to go to God in prayer unless our circumstances drive us to our knees. Sometimes, prayer is something we do only when we come to the end of ourselves. But James wants us to know that while it is good and proper to pray during tough times, it's a sign of spiritual maturity to praise God during the good times.

Though many people cry out to God during hard times, some actually withdraw from fellowship with the Father during trying circumstances. Just when they need God most, they pull away from him. God is not merely our heavenly Father; he is truly our heavenly Daddy, and we are his children. As children of God, we need to realize that we can always go to our heavenly Daddy whenever we are frightened, anxious, confused, uncertain, doubtful, or feeling guilty and ashamed over sin.

Why some Christians withdraw from God

Why do some Christians, in times of crisis or suffering, actually put *more* distance between themselves and the Lord instead of turning to him for help? Why do they withdraw from prayer and fellowship with God? Why do they feel they can't bring their honest emotions and pain into God's presence? I think there are two possible reasons why some Christians withdraw from God.

First, I think many Christians have the wrong concept of suffering. They believe that if life has dealt them a painful blow or a setback, then it must be because God is angry with them. So, just as children often avoid an angry parent, Christians sometimes avoid God if they think he is angry with them.

Some Christians have never internalized God's grace for their lives. They have committed their lives to Christ, they are saved by grace, they are born again—but they don't accept the reality of God's grace. They have never let go of the feelings of guilt, shame, and inadequacy they feel because of their past sins. God is chasing after them, trying to gather them in his arms and tell them, "All is forgiven! My Son Jesus paid the full price of your sins." But they think he's chasing them to punish them. So they run from him like guilty, frightened children. Just when they need their loving Father the most, they hide from him.

Second, many people avoid prayer and fellowship with God because they are angry with God. They are going through a difficult time—a loss, a crisis, an illness, an injury, a financial setback, a strained or broken relationship—and they blame God for those hurtful circumstances. As a result, they want nothing to do with God because they think he is ruining their lives.

Satan enjoys putting distance between us and the Lord. Once Satan is able to convince you that God doesn't love you, that God does not have your best interests at heart, he has you right where he wants you. The devil will eagerly exploit that opportunity. Once he has driven a wedge between you and God, he can convince you to rationalize any act of rebellion, any act of sin. He'll have you convinced that you are justified in doing anything you want to do—no matter how evil—as a way of getting back at God. You will rationalize it because, in your mind, God doesn't love you.

I remember a conversation I had a few years ago with a psychiatrist who counseled teenagers. He told me, "I have seen a common pattern in all the teenagers I work with who are engaging in drugs, alcohol, or illicit sex. They have all convinced themselves that their parents don't love them. Once they are convinced they are unloved, they feel justified in doing anything they want."

And I've observed that some Christians follow that same pattern. They convince themselves, "Well, God doesn't love me—he didn't answer my prayer. My life is a disaster. Nothing works out for me. Obviously, God doesn't love me." And once a Christian begins thinking this way, he or she is immediately in the clutches of the devil.

Mature Christians do not let Satan drive a wedge between them and their Lord. They refuse to allow the circumstances of life to affect their fellowship with God. They cling to God for dear life.

In Acts 16, Paul and Silas were in Philippi, a Roman colony in eastern Macedonia, when they exorcised a demon from a servant girl and angered the slave-masters who owned her. Her owners would no longer be able to make a profit from her demonic utterances. So the slave-masters dragged Paul and Silas before the magistrate, and the magistrate had the two missionaries beaten with rods, then tossed into prison and fastened in stocks.

Well, you can imagine how Paul and Silas must have reacted to being treated so unfairly by the Philippian authorities—and by God, who allowed it to happen. If we turn to Acts 16, we can expect to read: "As Paul and Silas languished in prison, their backs raw and bleeding from the rods, they moaned and complained. Refusing to pray, they moped and grumbled bitterly to each other about the unfairness of God, who allowed them to suffer after they had served him so faithfully by preaching the gospel."

Hmm. I've looked throughout Acts 16, and I can't find those words anywhere. Instead, the account tells us, "About midnight Paul and Silas were praying and singing hymns to God, and the prisoners were listening to them" (v. 25). Instead of withdrawing from God and complaining about God, they were clinging to God for dear life. They were praying. They were singing songs of joy! And they were witnessing for Christ, because the other prisoners were listening to them.

Cling to God when times are tough

Spiritually mature Christians cling to God in hard times. No matter what the world may do to us, our joy and fellowship with the Lord should remain strong and unaffected. If anything, tough times should draw us closer to God—not drive us away. Clinging to the Lord in tough times offers three advantages to us as believers:

First, fellowship with God is an antidote to loneliness. Jesus promised he would never leave us or forsake us. Cling to that promise and you will never be lonely.

Second, fellowship with God reminds us that he is in control. We easily lose sight of God's sovereignty as we look at all the problems and crises in our lives and all around us. By clinging to God through prayer and praise, we are reminded that, no matter what happens, the Lord is in control.

Third, fellowship with God helps us to see our lives from God's perspective. When we look at our circumstances and our problems from our ground-level perspective, they seem to tower over us, immense and unconquerable. But when we look at those same circumstances and problems from God's heavenly perspective, we realize that we can do all things through Christ who strengthens us.

George Mallory and Andrew "Sandy" Irvine were mountain

climbers who made several attempts to scale Mount Everest in the 1920s. During the 1924 British Mount Everest Expedition, they sought the summit of the highest mountain in the world from the northeast ridge. Other members of the expedition spotted them just a few hundred yards from the summit, and many Everest historians believe Mallory and Irvine actually made it to the top of the world, almost thirty years before it was officially conquered by Edmund Hillary and Tenzing Norgay. No one will ever know for sure, because Mallory and Irvine didn't come back alive (their remains were not found until seventy-five years later).

After the two climbers disappeared, the rest of the expedition party returned to England in defeat. One of the survivors described the ill-fated venture in a speech to an audience in London. Pointing to a large photograph of Mount Everest on the wall behind him, he reportedly said, "Mount Everest, you defeated us once; you defeated us twice; you defeated us three times. But Mount Everest, we shall someday defeat you, because you can't get any bigger and we can."[26]

Our afflictions may look as unconquerable as Mount Everest, but they can never grow bigger than God allows. But, by the grace of God, *we can grow bigger than our afflictions.* We can grow bigger by God's grace, through his power, if we cling to him and continue to remain in fellowship with him. As the prophet Isaiah reminds us,

> they who wait for the LORD shall renew their strength;
> they shall mount up with wings like eagles;
> they shall run and not be weary;
> they shall walk and not faint.
> (Isaiah 40:31)

What is the Mount Everest that confronts you today? Whatever it may be, face it squarely right now, and say, "You can't grow any bigger—but by God's grace, I can. I claim God's power, wisdom, and strength, and I will conquer you."

In 1855, Irish poet Joseph M. Scriven composed the hymn

"What a Friend We Have in Jesus" to comfort his mother when he left Ireland and moved to Canada. Scriven was no stranger to sorrow. Twice he was engaged to be married. His first engagement ended in the drowning death of his fiancée the night before they were to wed. His second engagement ended in his fiancée's death due to pneumonia. After these two tragedies, Scriven remained unmarried. He devoted the remainder of his life to serving Christ and helping others. The words of "What a Friend We Have in Jesus," originally written to comfort his mother, have given spiritual solace to millions over the decades since he wrote them:

> What a Friend we have in Jesus,
>   all our sins and griefs to bear!
> What a privilege to carry
>   everything to God in prayer!
> O what peace we often forfeit,
>   O what needless pain we bear,
> All because we do not carry
>   everything to God in prayer.
> Have we trials and temptations?
>   Is there trouble anywhere?
> We should never be discouraged;
>   take it to the Lord in prayer.
> Can we find a friend so faithful
>   who will all our sorrows share?
> Jesus knows our every weakness;
>   take it to the Lord in prayer.
> Are we weak and heavy laden,
>   cumbered with a load of care?
> Precious Saviour, still our refuge,
>   take it to the Lord in prayer.
> Do thy friends despise, forsake thee?
>   Take it to the Lord in prayer!
> In His arms He'll take and shield thee;
>   thou wilt find a solace there.

Blessed Saviour, Thou hast promised
Thou wilt all our burdens bear;
May we ever, Lord, be bringing
all to Thee in earnest prayer.
Soon in glory bright unclouded
there will be no need for prayer,
Rapture, praise and endless worship
will be our sweet portion there.

I think we in the twenty-first-century church miss much of the accumulated wisdom and comfort of past Christian eras by forsaking some of the great hymns. We need to be reminded weekly, if not daily, that the Lord Jesus truly bears our sins and griefs, that he is truly our refuge in times of trouble, and that he takes us and shields us in his arms.

We need to be reminded, day after day, that if we are suffering, we should immediately go to the Lord in prayer. If we are cheerful, we should sing his praises. In good times and in hard times, we should cling to the Lord Jesus Christ for dear life.

Offer intercessory prayer for others

In verses 14 and 15, the apostle James tells us:

> Is anyone among you sick? Let him call for the elders of the church, and let them pray over him, anointing him with oil in the name of the Lord. And the prayer of faith will save the one who is sick, and the Lord will raise him up. And if he has committed sins, he will be forgiven (5:14-15).

Prayer serves several specific purposes, and one of these purposes is to deal with disease and to raise up those who are sick. A person who is ill is usually too sick to attend church and must therefore call the elders to anoint him or her with oil and pray. In the first century, doctors used olive oil as a medicine, so the anointing with oil symbolized a partnership between the healing power of God and the healing arts of doctors and their remedies. Oil is also used throughout the Bible as a symbol of the Holy Spirit. So when the elders anoint the sick with oil, the anointing signifies the church's acknowledgment that healing power comes from God through the ministry of the Holy Spirit.

There is confusion in the church today over this statement in verse 15, "And the prayer of faith will save the one who is sick." Who offers up the prayer of faith? The elders. Yet I have seen many occasions where a sick person has been prayed for and anointed, and when he or she did not experience immediate healing, someone said to that person, "You must not have enough faith. If you had sufficient faith, you would have been healed."

That is unbiblical theology, and it is cruel and hurtful to the person who is sick. It is not up to the sick person to summon up a sufficient quantity of faith for his own healing. It is the elders who are to pray and act in faith.

It breaks my heart when I see a so-called faith healer on television saying that if you send a donation of so many dollars to his ministry, you will experience a divine healing. If a person makes a donation but is not healed, then the charlatan heaps more guilt on the sick person, saying, "Well, it's your own fault! You just didn't have enough faith to be healed."

I'm not saying that the faith of the sick person plays no part in the healing process. In the gospel accounts, we read of several instances where Jesus told the person who was healed, "Your faith has made you well." Mark 5 tells the story of a woman who had suffered from bleeding for twelve years, and after spending all she had on doctors, she only got worse. So she followed Jesus, reached out and touched his garment, and immediately she was healed. And Jesus turned to her and said, "Daughter, your faith has made you well; go in peace, and be healed of your disease" (Mark 5:34). And when Jesus healed a blind beggar, Bartimaeus, in the village of Jericho, he told the man, "Go your way; your faith has made you well" (Mark 10:52).

But that is not the situation the apostle James describes here. He is speaking about a person who is too sick to leave his home and is ministered to by the elders of the church. It is the elders who pray over him, and it is the elders' faith that is the channel for God's healing power in the sick person's life.

What is the prayer of faith? It is the belief, expressed in prayer by the elders of the church, that our sovereign God is in the business of healing people. It is also the belief that the option to heal remains in the hands of God. We do not give orders to God as if he were a genie in a bottle. He is the Almighty God, and we must respect his sovereign will. God has a *prerogative* to heal, not an *obligation* to heal. Our obligation as believers is to petition God, to trust in him, and to accept his sovereign will.

Many Christians are also confused about this line in James 5:15: "And if he has committed sins, he will be forgiven." People sometimes misinterpret this as a blanket statement that illness is the result of sin. Some illnesses do result from sin, and that's why James says, "*If* he has committed sins..." But that is a big if. We live in a fallen world, and disease is a result of the fallenness of this world. But disease is not necessarily the result of a specific sin in the life of the sufferer. It is unbiblical to assume that a person's illness is caused by sin.

Prayer releases the power of God

In verses 16 through 18, James gives us a set of guidelines for releasing the power of God through prayer:

> Therefore, confess your sins to one another and pray for one another, that you may be healed. The prayer of a righteous person has great power as it is working. Elijah was a man with a nature like ours, and he prayed

fervently that it might not rain, and for three years and six months it did not rain on the earth. Then he prayed again, and heaven gave rain, and the earth bore its fruit (5:16-18).

What does James mean when he says, "Confess your sins to one another"? Some people interpret this to mean that Christians should get together and hang out all their dirty laundry so that everyone will know all the sins they have committed. This is a fashionable pastime in some Christian circles. I know of one group in California that practiced the "dirty laundry" approach to confession—and several marriages were destroyed by the revelations!

Some would say that group sharing in "total honesty" brings relief. But this is not genuine honesty. It is a dropping of all boundary lines in our relationships with others. There might be a feeling of catharsis, but the feeling is temporary—and is often followed by a sense of embarrassment or shame because things that were meant to be private are now exposed. What has been said can never be unsaid.

There is a place for being accountable to other believers. There is a place for fellowship with other believers that involves praying for one another, encouraging one another, sharing each other's burdens, and asking others to hold us accountable for growth in some area of our lives.

But that does not mean we should hang out our sins for all to see. Telling everyone your sins will accomplish only two things in your life: First, it will cause you to be focused on your sins, not on God. Second, because you are focused on your sins instead of God's power, Satan will find it much easier to tempt you back into your old life of sin. So what does James mean when he says "confess your sins to one another"?

Confessing our sins to one another

First, we know that confession begins with God because every sin we commit is ultimately a sin against God. As the psalmist said,

"Against you, you only, have I sinned and done what is evil in your sight" (Psalm 51:4a). And in 1 John 1:9, we read, "If we confess our sins, he is faithful and just to forgive us our sins and to cleanse us from all unrighteousness."

Second, we must confess our sins to those who are directly affected by them. In the Sermon on the Mount, Jesus said that before we make our offering to the Lord, we need to make sure we have made things right with anyone we have sinned against. "So if you are offering your gift at the altar and there remember that your brother has something against you, leave your gift there before the altar and go. First be reconciled to your brother, and then come and offer your gift" (Matthew 5:23-24). And the apostle Paul said that we should live tolerantly toward one another, "bearing with one another and, if one has a complaint against another, forgiving each other; as the Lord has forgiven you, so you also must forgive" (Colossians 3:13).

Third, we should never confess our sins beyond the circle of influence of our sins. Private sin requires private confession to the individual who was wronged. Why is it so important for us to confess our sins to God and to those we've sinned against? Why is confession critical for releasing God's power in prayer?

There are several important reasons: Unconfessed sin places a barrier between us and God. It puts a strain on our fellowship with the Father. When we confess our sins to God, we draw close to him once more. Confession causes us to realize that we can start afresh with God. It prevents us from getting bogged down in guilt and shame. When we keep short accounts with God, we remain effective in our ministry for God. Moreover, confessing our sins to God and to those we have offended is essential for our spiritual growth. We cannot grow spiritually while taking a casual attitude toward sin.

Some of us find it difficult to confess our sins to God and others. What prevents us from confession?

One factor is *pride*. No one likes to say, "I was wrong." It makes us feel vulnerable to say, "Please forgive me." Something about the prideful human spirit equates confession with weakness. As we grow more spiritually mature, we come to realize that it's a sign of strength to honestly admit our flaws and to ask forgiveness from those we have offended.

Another factor is *fear*. Some of us fear that if we say, "I sinned against you, please forgive me," the other person will withhold forgiveness. If you have ever asked for forgiveness from someone, only to be harshly rebuffed, then you know how much that hurts. Confessing sin is an act of vulnerability. We open ourself to being hurt when we ask for forgiveness. But it's a risk worth taking, and spiritual maturity requires that we overcome our timidity and fear, and that we dare to be hurt in order to be obedient to Christ.

Yet another factor is *dishonesty*. Sometimes, when we know deep down that we are wrong, that we have sinned, we want to hide the truth from ourselves or from God or from the person we have wronged. Like Adam and Eve hiding in the garden, or like Cain lying to God about the murder of his brother Abel, we try to cover up our sin instead of facing it squarely and dealing with it once and for all. As long as we are dishonest about our sin, it remains a barrier to fellowship with God and others.

Why does James teach us that it is essential to confess our sins and pray? He gives us the answer in verse 16: "that you may be healed." What kind of healing does James refer to here? He is speaking of mended relationships with others and a healed fellowship with God.

I have found this principle to be true in my own life: I cannot preach, I cannot minister, I cannot pray, I cannot carry on any ministry for Christ as long as I have unconfessed sin in my life. This is true whether I have sinned against God alone or have offended another person.

Why is my prayer life powerless when there is unconfessed sin in my life? The last line of verse 16 tells us: "The prayer of a righteous person has great power as it is working." When we harness the power of prayer, it becomes an incredible force for blessing and ministry in our lives. But how can we have access to God's power through prayer when our fellowship with him is broken because of sin?

Elijah and the power of prayer

James goes on to remind us of the Old Testament prophet Elijah: "Elijah was a man with a nature like ours, and he prayed fervently that it might not rain, and for three years and six months it did not rain on the earth. Then he prayed again, and heaven gave rain, and the earth bore its fruit" (5:17-18). Elijah knew how to harness the power of prayer. He knew that the prayer of a righteous man could achieve much.

You find the story of Elijah in 1 Kings 17 and 18. It's the story of how Elijah learned to release the power of God through prayer. When evil King Ahab and his wicked wife, Jezebel, ruled Israel, they led the nation into moral compromise and apostasy. Because the nation had fallen away from God, Elijah prayed that there would be no rain in Israel for three and a half years. And God answered Elijah's prayer.

That long drought was a national disaster, and a judgment against the false god Baal. God permitted this calamity to fall upon Israel in order to teach the evil king, the queen, and all their followers that the God of Israel will not be mocked. He will be obeyed. At the end of the three and a half years of drought, Elijah challenged the prophets of Baal to a confrontation to demonstrate once and for all which was the true God and which was false.

Elijah summoned the 450 prophets of Baal and 400 prophets of Asherah to the top of Mount Carmel. With total confidence in the God of Israel, Elijah said to them, "Let two bulls be given to us, and let them choose one bull for themselves and cut it in pieces and lay it on the wood, but put no fire to it. And I will prepare the other bull and lay it on the wood and put no fire to it. And you call upon the name of your god, and I will call upon the name of the LORD, and the God who answers by fire, he is God."

Beginning in the morning and continuing till noon, the prophets of Baal cried out, "O Baal, answer us!" They wailed and danced and chanted in screams. But no word, no rumbling, no fire came from the god of thunder and lightning.

To demonstrate his confidence in God, Elijah began to rub it in. "Cry aloud," he mocked, "for he is a god. Either he is musing, or he is relieving himself, or he is on a journey, or perhaps he is asleep and must be awakened."

As Elijah taunted the prophets of Baal, they whipped themselves into a frenzy. They cut themselves with knives and bled profusely. They pleaded for Baal to send fire, but he didn't send a single spark. They raved on and on, but there was not a flicker of response.

Then it was Elijah's turn. He calmly rebuilt the altar of the Lord, which had fallen into disrepair. Then he had the people fill four large jars with water and drench the sacrificial bull and the firewood. Then he had them bring four more jars of water and drench it again. And then four more jars of water to drench it a third time. And the water was pooled in the altar and the trench around it. The altar was soaked. Clearly, it would be impossible to light a fire on that altar.

But Elijah had confidence—not in himself, because he knew all too well his own fears and weaknesses. No, Elijah's confidence was in Yahweh, the "God of Abraham, Isaac, and Israel." He knew his God would not let him down.

Before going on with the story, how are you doing in the trust department? Do you ask God for miracles? And when you ask him for supernatural intervention, do you try to make things easy for him and ask only for tiny, insignificant miracles? Or, like Elijah, do you have such trust in God's power that you ask him to do things that are wildly impossible?

Elijah had no intention of making things easy for God. He gave God a triple challenge, drenching the altar with water three times before asking God to send fire from heaven. And then he prayed—and his prayer was surprisingly solemn and understated:

"O LORD, God of Abraham, Isaac, and Israel, let it be known this day that you are God in Israel, and that I am your servant, and that I have done all these things at your word. Answer me, O LORD, answer me, that this people may know that you, O LORD, are God, and that you have turned their hearts back" (1 Kings 18:36-37).

The moment Elijah finished praying, a megabolt of fire flashed from the sky and ignited the animal sacrifice and the altar. The blast was so hot that it even consumed the stones and vaporized the water. And all the people knew without any doubt that the God of Israel was the one true God.

And the awestruck people chanted in fear, "The LORD, he is God; the LORD, he is God." Then, because the sin of idolatry and blasphemy had to be dealt with and removed from the land, Elijah ordered that the prophets of Baal be rounded up and executed.

Elijah warned the evil King Ahab that the rains were coming. And Elijah went up on Mount Carmel and bowed before God—then sent his servant to look toward the sea for a sign of approaching rain. The servant reported, "There is nothing there." Elijah said, "Go again." This happened seven times, and not once in all those times did Elijah become discouraged, nor did he doubt that the rains would come. The seventh time the servant looked to the sea, he saw an approaching cloud. Then Elijah sent the servant to warn Ahab to get out his umbrella, and a violent rainstorm fell upon the land. "And the hand of the LORD was on Elijah," the Scriptures conclude.

Elijah prayed the will of God, and he trusted the timing of God. Now notice what James tells us about Elijah: "Elijah was a man with a nature like ours…" In other words, he was as human as any of us. He was no better, no worse, than you or me. His prayers were answered because he prayed according to the will of God. He trusted God, he believed God, and he waited upon God.

Elijah is the example James sets before us. He is our role model of faithful prayer.

Pray that you and your fellow believers will remain faithful

Finally, in verses 19 and 20, the apostle James urges us to pray for one another that we would remain true and faithful to the Lord Jesus Christ:

> My brothers, if anyone among you wanders from the truth and someone brings him back, let him know that whoever brings back a sinner from his wandering will save his soul from death and will cover a multitude of sins (5:19-20).

Do you know someone who has wandered from the truth? Do you know someone who has turned his or her back on the Word of God? Do you know someone who has drifted away from the fellowship of God's people?

Please pray for that person. Don't give up on that brother in Christ. Don't surrender the soul of that sister in Christ. Go before God and lift that person up to him, asking God to reach out to that wandering soul and call that person back to himself.

Prayer is incredibly powerful, more powerful than you can imagine. The power of prayer is literally the power that spoke the universe into existence. The power of prayer is literally the power that brought the Lord Jesus out of the tomb. This power is limitless—and it is available to you. Hearts can be changed, the lives of men and women and children can be redirected, by the power of prayer alone.

And when you pray, you will find that God will fill your heart with love for that person. And through your prayers, you will help to bring back a sinner from his wandering, and you will help to save a soul from death.

Your prayers will cover a multitude of sins.

Love does not sweep sins under the carpet. Where there is love, there is truth. Where there is truth, there is honest confession of sin. Where there is confession of sin, there is cleansing and forgiveness from God.

In his book *Victory in Spiritual Warfare*, Dr. Tony Evans tells the story of being trapped in an elevator in a high-rise building. The elevator was stuck between floors, the doors wouldn't open, and as soon as his fellow passengers realized they couldn't get out, they began to panic. "Some cried," he recalled, "some yelled out for help, and some started banging hard on the door."

As the other people panicked, Evans noticed the emergency phone next to the door. So he made his way to the phone, picked it up, and waited for someone to answer. Finally, a voice on the line said, "Is there a problem?"

"Yes, sir," Evans said, "we are trapped. Can we get some help?"

"We'll be right there."

You and I often feel trapped. We may feel trapped by our own illness or the illness of someone we love. We may feel trapped by our financial circumstances. We may feel trapped by sins and mistakes of the past. We may feel trapped by the opposition or scornful behavior of other people. We may feel trapped by an addiction or a destructive habit.

When we are trapped, our first impulse is to panic, to lose our heads, to start pounding and shouting and imagining the worst. But no matter what the circumstances that seem to have us trapped, there is a phone we can pick up. Someone is always there on the line. Help is always available.

That phone is called prayer. And its limitless power is always available, twenty-four hours a day, seven days a week.

Prayer can move mountains, transform hearts, save wandering souls from death, and cover a multitude of sins. Pray in both good times and hard times. Pray for yourself and pray for others. Pray that you remain faithful throughout your life. Pray to unleash the infinite power of God.

Take it from Old Camel-Knees. The prayer of one righteous person has the power to work wonders. So be that one righteous person who prays—and then stand back and watch God work!

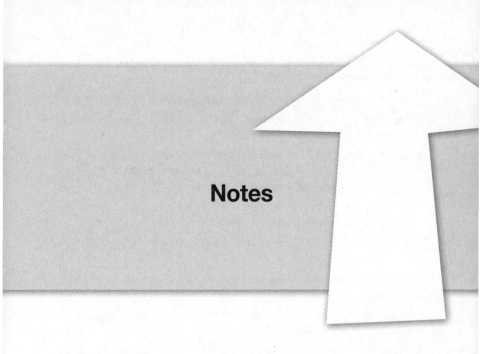

Notes

1. Keith Miller and Bruce Larson, *The Edge of Adventure: An Experiment in Faith* (Waco, TX: Word, 1974), 29.

2. George MacDonald, *Unspoken Sermons*, Series One, "The Consuming Fire" (Seattle: CreateSpace, 2011), 15.

3. Charles R. Swindoll, *The Darkness and the Dawn* (Nashville: Thomas Nelson, 2006), 221.

4. James Stuart Bell, *The One Year Men of the Bible: 365 Meditations on the Character of Men and Their Connection to the Living God* (Carol Stream, IL: Tyndale, 2008), entry for February 3.

5. Thomas Powers, "How the Battle of Little Bighorn Was Won," *Smithsonian* magazine, November 2010, www.smithsonianmag.com/history-archaeology/How-the-Battle-of-Little-Bighorn-Was-Won.html?c=y&page=8.

6. Francis M. Cosgrove, *Essentials of Discipleship* (Dallas: Roper Press, 1988), 74-75.

7. Dennis J. DeHaan, *Windows on the Word* (Grand Rapids, MI: Baker Books, 1984), 96-97.

8. Charles Colson, *Loving God* (Grand Rapids, MI: Zondervan, 1996), 92.

9. Joseph Stowell, *The Weight of Your Words: Measuring the Impact of What You Say* (Chicago: Moody, 1998), 39.

10. Bennett Cerf, "Trade Winds," *The Saturday Review*, December 22, 1951, 4, www.unz.org/Pub/SaturdayRev-1951dec22-0000.

11. Bell, *The One Year Men of the Bible*, entry for June 19.

12. Terri Gibbs, editor, *Our Daily Bread: Collector's Edition II* (Nashville: Thomas Nelson, 2005), 114.

13. "Carl Sandburg's Lincoln Comments," *Abe's Blog Cabin: The Life and Legacy of Abraham Lincoln and the Civil War Era*, December 25, 2009, http://abes blogcabin.org/carl-sandburgs-lincoln-comments.

14. Daniel Webster Whittle, "Hold the Fort," 1870, En.Wikisource.org, http://en.wikisource.org/wiki/Hold_the_Fort.

15. John Timbs, *English Eccentrics and Eccentricities* (London: Chatto and Windus, Piccadilly, 1875), 76.

16. "Hold the Fort!," words and music by Philip Paul Bliss, 1870, in the public domain.

17. Bruce Larson, *Luke: The Communicator's Commentary*, ed. Lloyd J. Ogilvie (Nashville: Thomas Nelson, 1983), 166-67.

18. Randy C. Alcorn, *Money, Possessions, and Eternity* (Wheaton, IL: Tyndale, 2003), 47.

19. Robert Rector and Rachel Sheffield, "Air Conditioning, Cable TV, and an Xbox: What Is Poverty in the United States Today?," Heritage.org, July 19, 2011, www.heritage.org/research/reports/2011/07/what-is-poverty.

20. Press release, "World Bank Sees Progress Against Extreme Poverty, But Flags Vulnerabilities," *The World Bank*, February 29, 2012, www.world bank.org/en/news/2012/02/29/world-bank-sees-progress-against-extreme -poverty-but-flags-vulnerabilities.

21. Tina Susman, "Lottery Winner Who Drew Outrage for Getting Welfare Is Found Dead," *Los Angeles Times*, October 2, 2012, http://articles.latimes .com/2012/oct/02/nation/la-na-nn-michigan-lottery-food-stamps-20121002.

22. Jen Doll, "A Treasury of Terribly Sad Stories of Lotto Winners," *Atlantic Wire*, March 30, 2012, http://news.yahoo.com/terribly-sad-true-stories-lotto-win ners-164423531.html.

23. Ibid.

24. Warren W. Wiersbe, *The Bible Exposition Commentary: New Testament, Volume 1: Matthew–Galatians* (Colorado Springs: Cook Communications, 2001), 379.

25. St. Jerome, *Lives of Illustrious Men*, Chapter II: James, www.ccel.org/ccel /schaff/npnf203.v.iii.iv.html.

26. Galen C. Dalrymple, "DayBreaks for 09/24/12—Getting Bigger," *Daybreak Devotions*, September 24, 2012, http://daybreaksdevotions.wordpress. com/2012/09/24/daybreaks-for-092412-getting-bigger/.

About Michael Youssef

Michael Youssef was born in Egypt and came to America in his late twenties in 1977. He received a master's degree in theology from Fuller Theological Seminary in California and a PhD in social anthropology from Emory University. Michael served for nearly ten years with the Haggai Institute, traveling around the world teaching courses in evangelism and church leadership to church leaders. He rose to the position of managing director at the age of thirty-one. The family settled in Atlanta, and in 1984, Michael became a United States citizen, fulfilling a dream he had held for many years.

Dr. Youssef founded The Church of The Apostles in 1987 with fewer than forty adults with the mission to "equip the saints and seek the lost." The church has since grown to a congregation of over three thousand. This church on a hill was the launching pad for Leading The Way, an international ministry whose radio and television programs are heard by millions at home and abroad.

For more on Michael Youssef, The Church of The Apostles, and Leading The Way, visit apostles.org and www.leadingtheway.org.

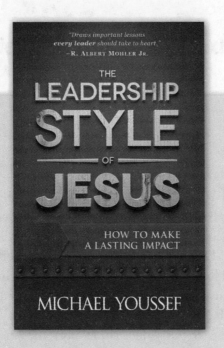

"Draws important lessons
every leader should take to heart."
–R. Albert Mohler Jr.

THE

LEADERSHIP
STYLE
—— OF ——
JESUS

HOW TO MAKE
A LASTING IMPACT

MICHAEL YOUSSEF

The Leadership Style of Jesus
How to Make a Lasting Impact

No matter what leadership arena you serve in—whether leading a family, a church, a civic organization, a company—adopting the leadership example of Jesus will make you more effective and productive. Leadership is influence, and no leader has had greater influence on the world than Jesus Christ. The lessons of His leadership style are practical, learnable skills that you can apply today.

Michael Youssef, who has executive experience in worldwide ministries, has examined the leadership Jesus modeled and suggests Christlike qualities every leader needs. But he doesn't stop there. With Jesus as the standard, Dr. Youssef considers how to deal with the temptations and pressures leaders face, including ego, anger, loneliness, criticism, the use of power, and passing the torch to others.

If you are in search of excellence in developing your leadership abilities, you will find much to aid your quest in this close-up look at Jesus—the greatest leader who ever lived.

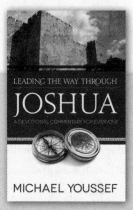

LEADING THE WAY THROUGH
JOSHUA
A DEVOTIONAL COMMENTARY FOR EVERYONE

MICHAEL YOUSSEF

LEADING THE WAY THROUGH
DANIEL

MICHAEL YOUSSEF

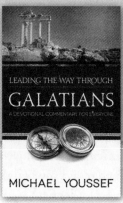

LEADING THE WAY THROUGH
GALATIANS
A DEVOTIONAL COMMENTARY FOR EVERYONE

MICHAEL YOUSSEF

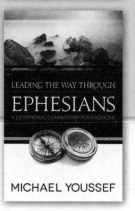

LEADING THE WAY THROUGH
EPHESIANS
A DEVOTIONAL COMMENTARY FOR EVERYONE

MICHAEL YOUSSEF

Leading the Way
Through the Bible Commentaries

About the Series: The Leading the Way Through the Bible commentary series will not only increase your Bible knowledge, but it will motivate you to apply God's Word to the problems of our hurting world and to a deeper and more obedient walk with Jesus Christ. The writing is lively, informal, and packed with stories that illustrate the truth of God's Word. The Leading the Way series is a call to action—and a call to the exciting adventure of living for Christ.

Books available:

Leading the Way Through Joshua
Leading the Way Through Daniel
Leading the Way Through Galatians
Leading the Way Through Ephesians

To learn more about Harvest House books and
to read sample chapters, visit our website:

www.harvesthousepublishers.com

HARVEST HOUSE PUBLISHERS
EUGENE, OREGON